Healing in the Hebrew Months

Exploring Hebrew Letters, Gematria, and their Musical Frequencies

Del Hungerford

All scriptures are paraphrased by the author. References to satan are in lowercase as he is not worthy of acknowledging with a capital letter.

Available from www.amazon.com, **www.healingfrequenciesmusic.com**, and other retail outlets where applicable.

ISBN-13: 978-1-7340956-0-9

Disclaimer

I am not a doctor, licensed dietitian or licensed counselor. The information in this book should not be seen as medical, nutritional, or mental health advice and is not intended to take the place of consulting licensed health care professionals. Check with your doctor, dietitian, counselor, and/or other health professional before implementing any of the suggestions outlined in this book.

Table of Contents

Introduction

This book came about solely by accident, or maybe, it was divine revelation. I'll let you, the reader, make that decision. I began an intriguing quest for the musical frequencies of the Hebrew letters, but I had no idea how many rabbit trails it would take to find the answer. Rabbit trails are wonderful, but when writing a book, picking and choosing what to include is quite the task. In the end, I included only the basic information about the actual musical frequencies of the Hebrew letters so that I could focus more on how those frequencies connected with the Hebrew months. The technical details are in another document (soon to be a book) available for download on the Healing Frequencies Music website.[1]

When I was asked to write the third book in this series, my first reaction was "why?" I couldn't see how the musical frequencies of the Hebrew aleph-bet had anything to do with healing. Even when Seneca first suggested that I do a song each month based on the Hebraic calendar, I thought connecting the frequencies with healing was a stretch. It took me a year to wrap my head around how to connect them. It took a chunk of time to compile notes for each month. After two years into the process, I began to see a pattern emerge between the Hebrew letters and each Hebraic month as I answered the call to write this book.

I didn't see the pattern as I recorded the song each month because I was only looking at that specific month. It was as if I were looking at the individual trees and not the whole forest. But once I collected and compiled everything, I saw it. I view the monthly cycle as walking a person through the Hebraic year with the focus of "leaving our personal Egypt" at the beginning of each year. It truly is a journey into health and healing—spirit, soul, and body. The cycle repeats year after year. As we mature, we leave behind what holds us back. Healing in the Hebrew months is more than physical healing. To a Jew, health includes their whole being. If we're healthy spiritually, the rest of our being will eventually line up.

Of course, I can't just throw a bunch of information at the reader without giving you a foundation. The first question people often ask is "How did you find the musical frequencies of the Hebrew letters?" I answer that question in this book. It's rather technical musical information, so I provide the truncated version so that most can understand. We take a walk down history lane to see how the Hebrew letters as we know them came to be. Then we look at various Jewish writings that are important in this musical frequency recipe. Next, a look at gematria paves the way to the common denominator for both musical frequencies and gematria—numbers. At this point, I explain my method (drum roll, please!) for the discovery of the musical frequencies of the Hebrew letters. Lastly, I present the basic information that I used for the first two years in the Song of the Month subscription and how that ties into the healing properties of the Hebrew months.[2]

Each Hebraic year builds on the year before so that we better ourselves by allowing the circumstances of our lives to mature us. Life circumstances do tend to fall within a cyclical pattern that mirrors the Hebrew months, which I discovered as I compiled information for this book. I called Seneca one day and shared my surprise at how the details of the eminent domain situation I was in the middle of just happened to be eerily like the monthly descriptions that she wrote about in her Times and Seasons Healing Box. (Cue creepy music here.) We work on this together, so she sends me copies of what goes out to the subscribers of the Times and Seasons

Healing Box, and I incorporate parts of that for the Song of the Month subscription.[3]

I discovered that life has cyclical patterns: patterns for health or unhealthiness. Our attitudes, behaviors, and words often determine how it all plays out. When we align our entire being with what God says about us, this is the first step into walking in divine health. We work out the rest through a process of maturity and character building. When coupled with developing intimacy with the Trinity, we become whole beings. The Hebraic year is meant to help the Jew become whole. As we follow the same patterns walked out by an established culture, we, too, can step into wholeness. Just as God walked beside the Israelites in and through their trials, he does so with us as well.

Join me on my journey into wholeness as we walk through healing in the Hebrew months by understanding the musical frequencies within the Hebrew letters, the living letters of the aleph-bet.

It's in the Series

This book is the third in a three-part collection covering the many facets of meaning found in the Hebrew months. Leah Lesesne wrote about the biblical significance of the months, including the emotional themes within each month. In part two, Seneca Schurbon of Freedom Flowers introduced you to the tribes, stones, gates, and constellations associated with each month. Here we are in part three, where I associate each month with the Hebrew letters, Hebrew gematria and musical frequencies.

I came onto the scene after the initial series began. Seneca called one day and said, "Hey, do you want to be part of our series?" My first response was less than enthusiastic. I was in the middle of moving after I'd lost my home to the eminent domain process. My mind was elsewhere, understandably so. Fast forward several months, my new home is mostly set up, I had time to think about my part, and here we are! It took me time to wrap my brain around how musical frequencies, Hebrew letters, and their gematria had anything to do with cycles of the Hebrew months.

Not that I wish to dwell on the early details, but it's time to recap how we got to this point. I include a quick synopsis of what's in the first two books because you really do want to read all of them to get the full picture of the cyclical patterns within the Hebrew months.

Healing in the Hebrew Months: Part 1

Leah Lesesne has a background in counseling and works as an inner healing practitioner. It only makes sense that she addressed the emotional themes of each month and the potential for healing when following the rhythm of a given month. Leah invented Captive Thought Therapy (CTT) for use in healing sessions. In part 1, she provides the reader with methods of working through trauma or situations during a given month. Leah also presented the foundational pieces necessary to understand the Hebrew calendar and the overall themes of each month. She provides scripture and prophecy, especially as it relates to Jesus as the messiah.

Healing in the Hebrew Months: Part 2

Seneca's book came out of her Times and Seasons Healing Box. In a dream, she was told that weeds have seasons, including times when they are vulnerable. She was informed in that dream that she shouldn't waste time and effort on the wrong weeds for the season. Her dream launched her into a three-year research project. That research led to explanations behind each Hebrew month, the original meaning of the corresponding constellations, the tribes that correlate to each, each tribe's stone, and the Gates of Jerusalem. These pieces all come together to provide strategy throughout the year as if God said, "Here's a basic blueprint you can follow." Blessings, areas of healing, potential pitfalls, and warfare are revealed when we align them all together. When we follow the times and seasons, it opens the door for specific blessings.

About a year into Seneca's introduction to the Times and Seasons Healing Box, she suggested that I create a monthly song subscription with a "guided visualization" for listeners to follow throughout each Hebrew month. I marinated in the idea for a year. I'm a teacher so coming up with a method of practicing a concept was easy! I piggyback on what I feel are key points in Seneca's writings and you'll see some of that here. Why do I do that? We have people who subscribe to the Times and Seasons Healing Box AND the Song of the Month. It's a method of creating two layers within a healing protocol.

Healing in the Hebrew Months: Part 3

My book focuses on the connection between Hebrew letters, their gematria, musical frequencies, and the A=432 concert pitch. The letters demonstrate the overall character of God and are meant to assist in our daily walk of intimacy with YHVH. As we learn to walk in that intimate place with him, we're at rest. That place of rest then gives our "being" more of an opportunity to heal.

I had an encounter where Jesus took me into the "look" of frequency. Some of that information is reflected in this book and the rest is for another time. Jesus showed me "beyond the veil" in the tabernacle where I watched the priest sing the names of God. As he sang, frequencies in the form of color ribbons, smoke, and sounds, floated around the Holy of Holies. Each frequency entangled with a Name of God while dancing about the room as it interacted with the stones on the priest's breastplate, the ark, and the mercy seat. It's fascinating to watch everything in the room vibrate and entangle with the singing of God's names. My enquiring mind wanted to know how it worked!

Taking this experience as a cue to dig further into the mysteries of the Hebrew letters and musical frequencies, I studied various "frequency and sound" connections. I have a doctoral degree in music but, some technical music details needed "dusting off within my brain." Revisiting historical and theoretical nuances concerning music brought back memories of college courses I didn't think were important at the time. As a performer, music theory and history took a back seat because I lived in a practice room. The non-musical research required wiggling down some tight rabbit holes that I never knew existed.

Seneca's book contains more information about the specific properties in each month than my book. I'd recommend adding her book to your collection so that you have a picture of how our monthly subscriptions work together. Leah's book provides an angle that reaches into the physical body as well as the emotions. If you need healing, Leah's book is a good place to start.

Now that I've primed the pump, we're ready to move onto and into how musical frequencies, Hebrew letters, and Hebrew gematria work within the cyclical pattern of the Hebrew months.
Enjoy the journey!

History of the Hebrew Letters

Experts hold many different opinions on the age of the Hebrew alphabet (aleph-bet). What we do know is that several alphabets evolved around the same time that looked similar. Before letters were formed, the ancients used pictographs (symbols). We see pictographs with a striking resemblance on cave walls all over the world. Symbols eventually morphed into a readable language.

A simple Google search for the word "pictograph" helps us see correlations in symbolic language. How's it possible that cultures that never intermingled with one another came up with similar drawings? Might I propose that when people have spiritual experiences, they envision similar things when their focus is on God? We'll save that deep discussion for another book. However, I will say that spiritual experiences are important in every culture.

Some archaeologists claim that many ancient sites were used as resonating chambers for toning during spiritual experiences. Acoustical specialists took measurements to show similar resonant frequencies at sites all over the world. John Reid, inventor of the cymascope, has an article on his website discussing his findings at the Great Pyramid of Giza.[iv] How would the ancients know to do such things?

A related science called archaeoacoustics first emerged in 1998.[v] A group of scholars from a variety of disciplines now meet in Malta every couple of years to present their findings on the acoustical properties of ancient sites. Many of the videos from various conferences are listed on the YouTube user's channel: SB Research Group.[vi] Type in the word "archaeoacoustics" in a Google or YouTube search to find a plethora of materials readily available on this topic.

You might wonder what this has to do with the history of the Hebrew letters. Glad you asked! Remember, I stated above that ancient languages came from pictographs. If you follow my thought process that ancients used pictographs to depict spiritual experiences, the Hebrew aleph-bet possibly came out of spiritual as well as daily life experiences. Many other cultures in the same region as the Hebrew nation have similar alphabets. It would make sense that cultures living among one another intermixed in a variety of manners. The Bible tells us this in stories of men marrying foreign women. This also indicates that their belief systems intermingled, which the Bible states. Archaeological evidence supports this too.

As to alphabets and spiritual experiences, the Hebrew culture also purports that their aleph-bet are living letters. They represent God (YHVH) and how he created the universe. When a Jew engages a letter, the purpose is to bring him closer to God. How is that possible, unless they believed these letters had special properties? The Jewish belief system concerning their alphabet hasn't changed. This is evident in their writings that span over at least two thousand years.

The discovery of the Dead Sea Scrolls gave the world insight into how a specific Jewish sect lived. In fact, "many biblical manuscripts closely resemble the Masoretic Text, the accepted text of the Hebrew Bible from the second half of the first millennium CE until today. This similarity is quite remarkable, considering that the Qumran Scrolls are over a thousand years older than previously identified biblical manuscripts."[vii]

Evidence shows little changed in biblical content over time. The website also states (above the previous quote) "About a dozen copies of some of these holy books were written in ancient paleo-Hebrew (the script of the First Temple era, not the standard script of the time)."[viii] Other scrolls were written in Aramaic and Greek. These writings show a progression of the Hebrew alphabet in a variety of copies of biblical texts. Scribes had to be exact when copying Biblical texts. Mistakes meant the entire text was thrown out. The Jews had to keep their religious writings from morphing over time.

Kabbalah, a form of Jewish mysticism founded around the Renaissance era, puts heavy weight on the living letters of the aleph-bet. Many of their teachings center on engaging with these letters to enhance spiritual experiences. Even before Kabbalah, other forms of Jewish mysticism existed. Much like we have various Christian denominations today, the Jewish community has a variety of sects within their religion.

We know the Hebrew aleph-bet did morph over time—from pictographs to an actual written language. The image below shows how the letter aleph (an ox head) changed into what we know today (Figure 1): First image = Early Hebrew/Early Semitic (20th century BCE). Second image = Paleo Hebrew/Middle Semitic (13th century BCE). Third image = Late Semitic/Square Aramaic Script (6th century BCE). Fourth image = Modern Semitic (10th century CE).[ix]

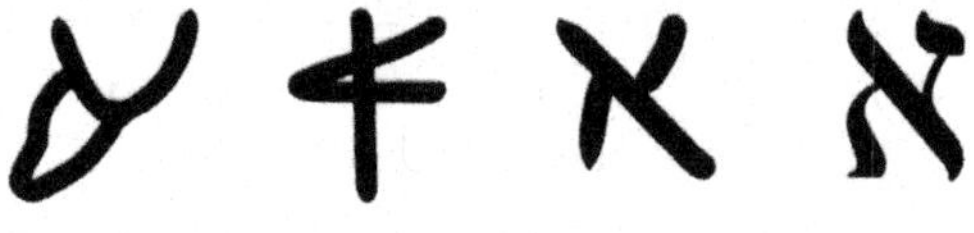

Figure 1

Research gives a timeline of how the Hebrew aleph-bet evolved. Additionally, pictures of cave writings, dates, and correlation to other cultures are added. Alphabets of other countries relate to the Hebrew aleph-bet, but I won't go into details here. If you want to study this topic further, you can find plenty of scholarly information online concerning these correlations.

In conclusion, one can see how an ancient alphabet is very important in the religious traditions of a culture and how it's remained consistent over time. Based on Jewish writings, the Hebrew aleph-bet is a living alphabet where one can engage with each letter to bring about a closer relationship with our Creator – YHVH – the one true name of God. (Figure 2: Letters are read from right to left)

יהוה

Figure 2

Kabbalah and the Sepher Yetzirah

Kabbalah is the mystical teachings of the Jewish faith. Kabbalah is defined as follows: "Inside your body breathes a person—a soul. Inside the body of Jewish practice breathes an inner wisdom—the soul of Judaism. We often call it 'Kabbalah,' meaning 'receiving.' Just as Jewish practice is received through an unbroken, ancient tradition from the revelation at Sinai, so is its soul. Kabbalah, then, is the received wisdom, the native theology and cosmology of Judaism."[x]

The modern Christian often considers Kabbalah a no-go zone. If we think the enemy (satan) has a hand in anything, we feel the need to stay away. But we often miss it because satan takes truth and twists it. For example, satan used Scripture to tempt Jesus during his forty days of fasting in the wilderness. Jesus knew his authority and used it to plow over the enemy through the simple declaration, "Get behind me, satan!" (See Matthew 16:23.)

If we're so concerned about being deceived by the enemy, then we don't understand our authority. Without getting into a denominational discussion concerning this issue, I'll simply say that the enemy is a copycat. If we look at what he's tried to hijack and dig through the muck to find the truth, we have nothing to fear. We're not given a spirit of fear, but of love, power, and a sound mind (2 Timothy 1:7). Many Christians won't look at new age practices because they're fearful of opening the door to the enemy.

Instead, we can practice covering ourselves, our imaginations, and the atmosphere around us with the light of God as we look at the Truth in the muck and mire of weirdness. The new age crowd has tapped into certain godly principles and knows how to use them. However, like mankind in general, it's often for the wrong purposes. I use the example of guns in many blog posts simply because it's a hot topic these days. Guns aren't bad in and of themselves. It's how people use them to create destruction that makes them harmful.

With that established, we move onto the Sepher Yetzirah. I'm not a fan of Wikipedia because the information isn't always accurate. However, their definition of the Sepher Yetzirah is one of the best I found: "Sēpher Yəṣîrâh, (Book of Formation, or Book of Creation) is the title of the earliest extant book on Jewish esotericism, although some early commentators treated it as a treatise on mathematical and linguistic theory as opposed to Kabbalah. Modern scholars have not reached consensus on the question of its origins."[xi]

Esotericism implies that information is only understood by a small group of people. That's obvious with the Sepher Yetzirah due to the variety of opinions about how to interpret it. Can anyone truly understand this work? Until the writing of this book, I didn't even know about the Sepher Yetzirah. I needed to understand which Hebrew letters coincided with the specific Hebrew months, so I did some historical research on the text. The earliest information concerning those details is found in the Sepher Yetzirah.

There are many versions of the Sepher Yetzirah. The Kabbalists took it on as one of their foundational writings during the Renaissance era. The original manuscript was written prior to Kabbalah. Although the author is unknown, many scholars agree on a date of the Talmudic period (about 1,300 CE) for the original manuscript. However, Wikipedia also states "according to Christopher P. Benton, the Hebrew grammatical form places its origin closer to the period of the Mishna, around the 2nd century CE."[xii]

According to most scholars, the Saadia version is the oldest and dates from the 10th century. The earliest surviving manuscript is a Geniza fragment dating from the 11th century. The Saadia version is primarily philosophical, rather than mystical, in nature. Along with commentaries, "this version had virtually no impact on subsequent kabbalists," suggests Professor Bryan Griffith Dobbs.[xiii]

You must understand that what we're using as a basis for our work in this book series pre-dates Kabbalah. Stories were passed aurally until a decent form of writing was established. Although there's no concrete proof of this, the Sepher Yetzirah is often attributed to Abraham. The evidence we have shows that Kabbalists began to use it as part of their belief system after it was written. Therefore, the Sepher Yetzirah is not Kabbalist writing. In this book, I refer to the earliest writing as a basis for my findings and musings.[xiv]

As we examine the correlation of the Hebrew letters with each month, we first see that reference in Chapter 6. Each simple letter is matched with a month, a position in the universe, and a body part. (See Figure 3.)

Sepher Yetzirah – Saadia Version (with Gematria added)

Month	Letter	Position in the Universe	Gematria
Nisan	Heh	Aries	5
Iyar	Vav	Taurus	6
Sivan	Zayin	Gemini	7
Tammuz	Chet	Cancer	8
Av	Tet	Leo	9
Elul	Yod	Virgo	10
Tishrei	Lamed	Libra	30
Cheshvan	Nun	Scorpio	50
Kislev	Samech	Sagittarius	60
Tevet	Ayin	Capricorn	70
Shevat	Tsadi	Aquarius	90
Adar	Qoph	Pisces	100

NOTE: months, letter, and position in the universe are found in chapter 6 of the Sepher Yetzirah

Figure 3

I only look at the correlation between the months and letters. Seneca Schurbon compared the other categories in part two of this book series. For that information, see her book Healing in the Hebrew Months: Prophetic Strategies Hidden in the Tribes, Constellations, Gates, and Gems available in paperback, Kindle and e-books throughout the internet.[xv]

My main question focused on how the writer of the Sepher Yetzirah paired the months with a specific letter. First of all, there are three categories of letters: mother, double, and simple. Chapter 1:3 spells out the position and purpose of each letter: "Twenty-two foundation letters: three mothers, seven doubles and twelve simples. Three mothers: Aleph, Mem, Shin: their basis is a scale of innocence and a scale of guilt and a tongue ordained to balance between the two. Seven doubles: Beth, Gimel, Daleth, Kaph, Peh, Resh, Tav. Their foundation is life and peace, wisdom and wealth, fruitfulness, grace and government. Twelve simples: Heh, Vav, Zayin; Cheth, Teth, Yod; Lamed, Nun, Samech; Ayin, Tzadi, Qoph. Their foundation is seeing, hearing, smelling, swallowing, copulating, acting, walking, raging, laughing, thinking, and sleeping."[xvi]

Each letter was assigned to a month, according to its position in the aleph-bet. Nisan is the first month, so the first simple letter (Heh) was assigned to that month. Iyar is the second month and was assigned the letter Vav, the next simple letter in the aleph-bet. The logical order continues through the last month, Adar, which is assigned the letter Qoph. As I looked at each month, the goal was to see if the properties of the assigned letter connected with the assigned month. I asked the following questions to test my theory: How did each month correlate with the meaning of the assigned letter? Are healing properties apparent in both? Is there a better positioning than what's assigned in the Sepher Yetzirah? Did the overall positioning make sense?

The answers to these questions are evident in the last part of this book where I provide a description of each month as it correlates to the assigned letter. In the Song of the Month subscription, I record spontaneous music based on the musical frequency of a specific Hebrew letter.xvii I was satisfied with the placement of letters and months as outlined in the Sepher Yetzirah because it worked quite naturally. That was evident as I recorded the voice-over activation each month. I've found it quite easy to harmonize the two in the monthly recordings.

Even before Kabbalah, other forms of Jewish mysticism existed. As far back as archaeological discoveries show, mysticism is inherent in every culture. Modern Christian thought turns mysticism into the stomping grounds of enemy territory because the new age movement has twisted "I AM" into its "all about me." New age thought says, "I am powerful through my own consciousness." Once the focus is no longer on God, we enter new age territory. Christian mysticism (if there's such a phrase) is all about following Jesus and doing what he did. He instructed us to do greater things than he did. All it takes is a walk through the New

Testament with a barometer checker into the life of Jesus. Uh, he did some pretty freaky stuff!

For those who may question Kabbalah or any other form of mysticism, get out the barometer checker and ask, "where's the focus?" When intimacy with God is the main goal without selfish gain, it's time to take a back seat and watch God move. Judge the fruit. What's good fruit will grow and flourish. What's rotten does what rotten things do – die. If we're concerned about deception, then we're walking in fear and not trusting God for his best. As you continue reading this book, consider my focus, especially in the activations. It's through intimacy with God – YHVH, his son Jesus, and the Holy Spirit that we should do all things. In him we live, move, and have our being. (Acts 17:28)

In conclusion, the Sepher Yetzirah is attributed to the Jewish culture and pre-dates Kabbalah. The assigning of a letter to each of the Hebrew months works quite well and follows a natural progression. These built-in healing properties—or what we call in our society today, preventative maintenance for health—are to benefit our spirit, soul, and body. We will explore this further in later chapters of this book.

Ancient Music History, Theory, and Culture

During my journey of discovery into the musical frequencies of the Hebrew letters, I found many others who blazed a similar trail. Most people looked at the cantillation marks, standard gematria, or a combination of other ways to find a method of how they believed music of the Bible was created. Richard Dumbrill is a scholar of ancient music. Wikipedia says that he "has devoted his academic career to the study of the archaeomusicology of the Ancient Near East, especially the interpretation of cuneiform texts of Music Theory written in

Sumerian, Babylonian and Hurrian."[xviii] I've had a couple of conversations with him via e-mail. He was kind enough to send me a copy of a paper titled "The Truth About Babylonian Music," which describes the translation of a cuneiform tablet with instructions for tuning ancient lyres around the time of David.

Richard Dumbrill notes in the video "Dumbrill on the Silver Lyre of Ur" that a musical system similar to what we know today wasn't used until around 1,000 BC. That would be about the time of David.[xix] When Dumbrill tunes the harp toward the end, he discusses how the process is all done through intervals. Those intervals are the most obvious ratios in the harmonic series (perfect fourths and perfect fifths). He comments that people understood harmonic laws at least five thousand years before Christ.

Since we know the ancient Sumerians used pictographs as their language, it wouldn't be a stretch of the imagination to see that the Israelites used pictures or even hand signals written on stone to depict musical ideas, notes, or tuning. Chironomy utilized hand signals and gestures to conduct and/or provide pitches. Zoltan Kodaly developed a method of hand signals still used in modern music education. If you've ever seen the *Sound of Music*, you've heard the lyrics to "Do-Re-Mi."[xx] That song is all about Kodaly hand signals. Each signal shows a musician the specific note of the scale to sing. The evidence of this practice dates as far back as the Egyptian culture in cave drawings.

Many musical factors need consideration when looking at historical information with only writings and archaeological evidence. Writings assist with the human side of the evidence (cultural norms, how people lived, etc.). I considered several pieces necessary in my process of discovering the musical frequencies of the Hebrew letters:

1) An understanding of the natural laws of musical harmonics (overtones series).

2) Historical musical practices and writings of the ancients BCE.

3) Music history in general.

4) The ability to read music well with a high-level knowledge of music theory.

5) Historical practices behind concert pitch.

6) Temperament: What is it? How does it work? How has it affected music history? Temperament also refers to tuning, how it was done, and how people dealt with this difficult issue.

7) Patterns between any of these.

8) Connections between music, nature, math, science, etc. or anything that connects.

9) Hebrew gematria: how it's used, why it's important, and how it all adds up (math).

I had to delve a bit deeper into music history, theory, temperament, concert pitch, and tuning before I began to see patterns. The more I research, the more I see that everything interconnects. I experimented with every form of gematria, thinking that I had to be missing something when nothing made sense. I knew to move on when I couldn't find a pattern or natural law.

Concerning tuning, musical notes change character and tuning based on the context of how and when they're used. As a clarinetist, I can hold a G in a rehearsal under varying chords. When that G is the fifth of a chord, it's super easy to tune. But the moment the chord changes and that same G becomes the third of the chord, I adjust to bring it down so that it's not sharp. It's the same note, but the context changes. Hebrew words follow the same pattern. Like music, adjustments will be needed, depending on how that letter is used in a word or sentence.

Concerning people and attitudes, part of the uniqueness of mankind is that we're created with a free will. Music making is a very personal experience and should allow artistic leeway in the creative process. As I imagined King David singing psalms and the high priest singing the names of God in the Holy of Holies, I understood these to be very personal encounters with God. Although the high priest entered the Holy of Holies on behalf of the people, he alone was in the presence of God.

Concerning concert pitch, I didn't try to make things fit into a specific concert pitch. I let the research take me down the rabbit trails as they appeared before me. When I was well into the work, I realized it was lining up with the A=432 concert pitch. (Concert pitch, sometimes called international standard pitch, refers to the pitch a group of instruments tune to for a performance. This pitch can vary, depending on the ensemble.)[xxi] For those who propose that A=444 is the divine concert pitch and tuning system to use, I've found no evidence of that yet. The musical frequencies of the Hebrew aleph-bet are closer to the A=432 concert pitch than any other.

In conclusion, I don't believe any musical culture expects something to be done the exact same way every time. Musicians who read and interpret sheet music never play it the same way twice. Music of the Hebrew letters is very personal for the musician. King David wrote the Psalms, but he did so out of inspiration. How many of us are in the same state of mind all the time? If we look at humanness as part of the equation for performing music from the Hebrew letters, the result won't be the same every time. Even when we write down the exact notes and rhythms, another musician's interpretation will be different. The intent of the musician is part of the musical recipe.

Hebrew Gematria

Gematria is a form of numerology. In this case, each letter of the Hebrew aleph-bet is given a number. There are many forms of gematria, but the most common is what we call standard gematria. Some of the Hebrew letters look different, depending on where that letter is placed within a word. These final forms are often given a different gematria when adding them to the end of the numerical system. In the Figure 4, I include each Hebrew letter, its standard gematria, and the A=432 concert pitch Hertz frequency using Pythagorean temperament. (Temperament is addressed in the next chapter, "Musical Frequencies of the Hebrew Letters.")

Hebrew letters with gematria and musical frequency in the A=432 concert pitch

Name	Letter	Gematria	Hertz A=432	Name	Letter	Gematria	Hertz A=432	Name	Letter	Gematria	Hertz A=432
Aleph	א	1	1	***Yod***	י	10	10.125	***Qoph***	ק	100	102.52
Bet	ב	2	2	***Kaf***	כ	20	20.25	***Resh***	ר	200	205.03
Gimel	ג	3	3	***Lamed***	ל	30	30.38	***Shin***	ש	300	307.55
Dalet	ד	4	4	***Mem***	מ	40	40.5	***Tav***	ת	400	410.06
Heh	ה	5	5.06	***Nun***	נ	50	51.26	***Final Kaf***	ך	500	512
Vav	ו	6	6	***Samech***	ס	60	60.75	***Final Mem***	ם	600	615.09
Zayin	ז	7	7.21	***Ayin***	ע	70	72	***Final Nun***	ן	700	729
Chet	ח	8	8	***Pe***	פ	80	81	***Final Pe***	ף	800	810.13
Tet	ט	9	9	***Tsadi***	צ	90	91	***Final Tsadi***	ץ	900	910.22

REMEMBER! Musical frequencies will vary slightly within a specific concert pitch and temperament depending on where that frequency is placed within a chord or scale.

Figure 4

Evidence of gematria used in the land of Canaan dates as far back as 1700 BCE. The dates are as follows:

- 1700 BCE – proto-Canaanite
- 1100 BCE – archaic Greek derived from proto-Canaanite
- 1050 BCE – proto-Canaanite to Phoenician
- 800 BCE – Early Hebrew – derived from Phoenician
- 700 BCE – Aramaic derived from Phoenician
- 650 BCE – Latin derived from Greek
- 200 BCE – Square Hebrew derived from Aramaic, adding the five letters with final forms[xxii]

Keep in mind that the Israelites lived in the land of Canaan between 1250–1050 BCE. Before 1700 BCE, according to records, the Israelites lived in Egypt, where those from other lands, including the Canaanites, visited on a regular basis. These cultures intertwined with one another, much like cultures co-mingle today. As such, the Israelites likely knew about and used gematria long before it was recorded.

I found other research on the musical frequencies of the Hebrew letters that require a variety of steps to make the system or method functional. But these methods didn't make sense to me because ancients created music to fit within the natural law of harmonics. They used a simple style that only required a good listening ear. Archeaomusicology shows this is the case. We didn't have an explanation of musical harmonics and how they worked until the time of Pythagoras (1500 BCE). But that doesn't mean people didn't use the laws of harmonic resonance prior to that date.

Jews began assigning numbers to letters thousands of years ago. What inspired them to do this? What was the purpose for doing so? Many scholars try to answer these questions, but I'm not sure it's totally possible. But we have a community of people who somehow figured out that assigning numbers to an alphabet was important. Jewish mystics tell of that importance as they discuss the Hebrew aleph-bet as "living letters." If they are living, an energy is associated with them. And energy equals frequency. When a belief is held and practiced consistently over thousands of years, it must hold some validity. When compared with modern practices and belief systems, we're lucky if we can keep a strong conviction for ten years, let alone more than three thousand years! Not much has changed in how the Hebrew culture views the use of gematria. We only have evidence of how it was used from 200 BCE on.

Part of my decision to tackle this monumental task involves what I share above. I used the long-held belief that the Hebrew aleph-bet is also represented by musical frequencies. Each letter tells a story, which then becomes a part of the interpretation of each word. Each letter carries a frequency, which, in turn, adds to the character of each word. You might be thinking *But the musical scale only has twelve notes and the Hebrew alphabet has twenty-two (or twenty-seven) letters.* Several of the letters are made up of other letters. Several letters also have the same fundamental frequency. However, this falls in line with what I stated above; some letters combine parts of other letters to make a new letter. When looking at this musically, we see the same type of relational overlap. But the context of how those musical frequencies are treated within the full word changes.

Some may think this fits in the land of "woo woo," where it's too far out to believe. Gematria is a form of numerology. But when numbers start connecting in several places (nature, math, geometry, etc.), I don't believe it's a coincidence. I see it as an invitation to look for the truth *in* something. Not everything extracted is truth because mankind tends to force concepts into pre-formed structures. Strong research requires looking objectively at a subject and throwing all pre-conceived ideas out the window. Look for the connections that fall together naturally. I took that approach with this project as I didn't want to force anything. I followed the numbers where they led me.

In conclusion, I propose that the Israelites understood gematria and its purpose earlier than currently thought. One of those purposes probably involved a musical representation of a letter, word, or phrase. Single frequencies, as well as full melodies (using gematria of sentences), might be present within these letters. As more excavations of ancient civilizations take place, more evidence may show up. Since the ancients didn't have technology as we know it today, they relied on what they witnessed in nature or received by divine inspiration. For example, consider the pyramids. Scholars can't seem to agree on how the ancients moved such large stones. What did they know that we do not understand today? I believe they understood energy and how to use it in ways we've never considered. We can't escape the modern technology box long enough to see other ways of accomplishing these tasks.

I can't ignore the obvious in my research—that gematria in the Hebrew alphabet lines up with specific musical frequencies in the A=432 concert pitch and the musical harmonic series. What are the odds of that? I don't believe it's a freak of nature. Somehow, this all fits within a divine plan, and in time, we'll understand how all these puzzle pieces fit so nicely together.

Musical Frequencies of the Hebrew Letters

When I began this research, I looked for a set method—one letter per pitch that matched gematria. That didn't work because everything I came up with sounded horrible and didn't fit within the natural laws of resonance, harmonics, and music theory. I then took a trip through the Torah to gather evidence. When the High Priest sang the names of God in the Holy of Holies and David sung the Psalms in the field as part of worship, neither of them looked at sheet music. Oh, wait. Sheet music wasn't invented yet. They had to use a way that still followed natural laws but also allowed for creativity, musical inspiration, and individuality.

Part of free will involves the ability to create through inspiration. Yes, natural laws govern how creativity works. However, freedom still exists within certain laws. We weren't created to be robots. By applying that thought process to this project, we see the law of harmonics and how it perfectly lines up with the Hebrew aleph-bet. Each Hebrew letter has a fundamental pitch. In the law of musical harmonics, all fundamental pitches have other pitches that resonate at varying strengths. In each fundamental pitch, every note of the musical scale is present. Some notes are more obvious than others. Musical timbre determines which harmonics are strongest in every sound-making device. This is how we can tell the difference between a flute and trumpet or a female from a male voice. Each person has their own special voice print. Voice recognition software can analyze harmonic details of a voice to a point that exceeds normal human hearing so that security doors will only open for that individual.

Since every musical note eventually shows up in each Hebrew letter, this appears to create a problem. Music has no absolutes, which brings us back to creativity. The creative part is deciding what order to place the notes. Some notes are more prominent than others and are the main notes to focus on when performing with the musical frequencies of the Hebrew letters. In a sense, it's like the fundamental note is the key signature. All the other notes focus around that "key" in order to create a harmonious musical experience. Even non-harmonic tones (notes not in the key signature) are usable.

The most important intervals are the first four in the harmonic series: perfect unison, perfect octave, perfect fifth, and perfect fourth. Nearly all music, except some Eastern music, is based on these four intervals. Musicologists have demonstrated that the ancient Sumerians used modal scales in their music through decoding cuneiform tablets. Even then, music was created using the natural laws of harmonics. As mentioned previously, a tuning manual exists from the time of David on a cuneiform tablet. It shows that all strings of the lyre were tuned to these natural harmonics (close to the A=439 concert pitch). The instrument was used to accompany singing. The tuning manual provides great insight into its use during David's reign.

I discovered a perfect correlation between the musical harmonic series and Hebrew gematria. Two forms of gematria are at play here: standard and small number. This makes sense because in the Hebrew culture, everything is based on layers or dimensions. For this book, I provide the correlation for the first nine Hebrew letters. The full chart is for sale separately, along with an audio teaching and demonstrations on the Healing Frequencies Music website.[xxiii] Since this book focuses on healing in the

Hebrew months, my goal is to introduce the basics of what I discovered. Two more harmonic series are present in the Hebrew letters. That information is all included in the teaching, "Musical Frequencies of the Hebrew Letters," that I mentioned above.

The chart (Figure 5) came about quite by accident or should I say divine discovery. What we often call accidental moments are more than likely divinely orchestrated.

- Column 1: The partial number in the harmonic series
- Column 2: Represents both the musical pitch and the Hebrew letter in standard gematria
- Column 3: Represents the small number gematria that matches the partial number
- Column 4: Musical frequencies in the A=432 concert pitch
- Column 5: Musical frequencies in the A=444 concert pitch for comparison
- Column 6: The partial number with its fundamental pitch (C) for the first nine letters of the Hebrew aleph-bet

Hebrew Gematria, Harmonic Series, and Hz Chart:

Partial Number	Standard Gematria	Small Number Gematria	Note Name to Hz in A=432	Note Name to Hz in A=444	Harmonic Series Note Assignment
1	1 = Aleph א	1	C = 1	C = 1.027	1 = C (series on C)
2	2 = Beth ב	2	C = 2	C = 2.055	2 = C
3	3 = Gimel ג	3	G = 3	G = 3.083	3 = G
4	4 = Dalet ד	4	C = 4	C = 4.111	4 = C
5	5 = He ה	5	E = 5.06	E = 5.203	5 = E
6	6 = Vav ו	6	G = 6	G = 6.16	6 = G
7	7 = Zayin ז	7	Bb = 7.21	Bb = 7.308	7 = Bb
8	8 = Chet ח	8	C = 8	C = 8.222	8 = C
9	9 = Tet ט	9	D = 9	D = 9.249	9 = D

Figure 5

The frequencies are based on the Pythagorean temperament or ratios. Standard gematria closely follows the harmonic series assigned note name for the A=432 concert pitch. In other words, the letter Tet is the ninth partial of the harmonic series that starts on C. Standard gematria is 9. The musical frequency is 9 Hz (D). The ninth partial in the harmonic series is also a D. This pattern repeats throughout the chart. That is surely no coincidence.

When comparing the A=432 concert pitch with A=444, the standard gematria numerical system is obviously closer to A=432 than A=444. Keep in mind that with these lower numbers, the distance from 8 Hz to 9 Hz is a whole step (C – D). 8.543 Hz is a C-sharp. These notes are almost two octaves lower than the lowest note on the piano. The Hertz numbers of third space C to fourth line D on the treble clef are a much greater distance than the two numbers: third space C (512Hz) and fourth line D (576Hz) and C-sharp (546.75Hz). It's all about ratios and wavelengths. To make sense of that, one must understand musical acoustics.

It's also important to note that frequencies within temperaments (adjusting the distance between each musical interval) will vary. For example, Gb/F# at 729 Hz is sharper than 700 Hz, but the note name is still the same. 700 Hz is flat enough that a good listener could hear that it's lower than 729 Hz. The distance between 720 Hz (just intonation) and 729 Hz (Pythagorean) is so minute, most people wouldn't be able to distinguish the two. In equal temperament, the same pitch resonates at 726 Hz. Depending on the temperament, a number will fluctuate up or down. I only mention this because these fluctuations tripped me up in the beginning stages of my research.

In Figure 6, I created a frequency chart based on Pythagorean ratios for the A=432 concert pitch as a reference point. Note: A different temperament will create small adjustments within the octave. Temperament is a form of measuring distance between notes just like inches and centimeters measure distance on a ruler.

C	1	2	4	8	16	32	64	128	256	512	1024	2048	4096	8192
C#/Db	1.0678	2.134	4.271	8.543	17.09	34.172	68.344	136.69	273.375	546.75	1093.5	2187	4374	8748
D	1.125	2.25	4.5	9	18	36	72	144	288	576	1152	2304	4608	9216
D#/Eb	1.2012	2.402	4.805	9.61	19.221	38.443	76.886	153.77	307.546	615.09375	1230.1875	2460.375	4920.75	9841.5
E	1.2656	2.53	5.06	10.125	20.25	40.5	81	162	324	648	1296	2592	5184	10368
F	1.333	2.666	5.333	10.666	21.333	42.666	85.33	170.665	341.33	682.66	1365.22	2730.64	5461.88	10922.56
F#/Gb	1.4238	2.847	5.69	11.39	22.78	45.56	91.125	182.25	364.5	729	1458	2916	5832	11664
G	1.5	3	6	12	24	48	96	192	384	768	1536	3072	6144	12288
G#/Ab	1.6018	3.203	6.407	12.814	25.629	51.258	102.515	205.03	410.06	820.125	1640.25	3280.5	6561	13122
A	1.687	3.375	6.75	13.5	27	54	108	216	432	864	1728	3456	6912	13824
A#/Bb	1.7777	3.555	7.111	14.222	28.444	56.888	113.777	227.555	455.111	910.222	1820.444	3640.888	7281.776	14563.552
B	1.8984	3.796	7.59	15.187	30.375	60.75	121.5	243	486	972	1944	3888	7776	15552

A=432 Concert Pitch with Pythagorean Ratios

In 14 Octaves

Healing Frequencies Music
www.healingfrequenciesmusic.com

Figure 6

In Figure 5, each letter is listed with the gematria and corresponding musical frequency. In order to understand why the frequencies are in the A=432 concert pitch, look for the number 432 in Figure 6. On this chart, 432 is the note A above middle C. On certain modern instruments (strings, fretted instruments, and some electronic keyboards), musicians may tune this A to 432 Hz. The remaining notes adjust automatically to that A. Should a musician decide to use equal temperament, ¼ comma mean-tone, or another temperament, the numbers between each octave vary slightly.

Until Rudolf Hertz, a German physicist, came along in the middle 1800's, the measurements in the charts I've provided for your reading pleasure didn't exist. Musicians tuned by ear using a single tuning fork, the town bell, a pitch pipe or what felt right. Prior to the industrial revolution, instrument makers built instruments according to the desires of the musician. There was no standard pitch until 1939! Our standard today is A=440.

Look again at Figure 6. It includes a list of A=432 musical frequencies starting from the number 1 in Pythagorean temperament. The list continues to 15,552 Hz (a full 14 octaves). Pythagorean temperament is based on natural ratios that the ancients understood. They didn't use our terminology, but they did have ears like we do.

Musicians tune by ear. They can hear the beating when notes are out of tune. When the pitch locks in tune with other musicians, the whole sound has a deeper resonance and sounds fuller. This is why opera singers can sing over an entire orchestra without a microphone. They've learned how to use their entire being to produce the needed resonance to project a big sound. As a clarinetist, I feel this resonance in my head because my teeth are in contact with the mouthpiece. Strong musicians temper pitches as they perform, paying close attention to how their notes line up with other musicians in the ensemble.

Note: Most listeners can't feel or hear a difference between A=440 and A=444 concert pitch because they are nearly identical. Musical instruments (other than electric keyboards) never stay at A=440 anyway. As an instrument warms up, some tend to play sharp while others go flat. To stay in equal temperament or within the A=440 concert pitch is difficult because natural forces (weather, humidity, etc.) affect tuning. Bottom line, all the hype about A=440 is exactly that—hype. However, some people are more sensitive to certain frequencies. What works well for one won't for another. No two bodies are alike.

The conclusion for this section is a bit more muddled than previous sections. I've presented a lot of technical musical information that most non-musicians often care to consider. However, it's important to understand that musical frequencies fluctuate, depending on concert pitch, temperament, and tuning. The chart in Figure 5 notes slight differences between some of the numbers. The remainder of the chart (not included) continues up the musical pitch ladder to show how Hebrew standard gematria lines up almost perfectly with musical frequencies in the A=432 concert pitch. If you're interested in learning more about that, feel free to purchase the teaching "Musical Frequencies of the Hebrew Letters" on the Healing Frequencies Music website. My purpose here is to show a general correlation, not examine fine details.[xxiv]

Next, we will discuss using these frequencies. In the next image (Figure 7), I show the first nine letters of the Hebrew aleph-bet, their musical pitches, and the first ten notes in the harmonic series from the fundamental note. The Hebrew letters are listed vertically on the left for the harmonic series that starts with the letter aleph. The fundamental pitch is C. Partials are numbered from 1 to 10 across the top. A *P* indicates a perfect interval (Perfect octave = P8, Perfect fifth = P5, Perfect 4th = P4). A capital *M* represents a major interval or in this case, a major second (whole step). A small *m* indicates a minor interval or in this case, minor third (three half steps), (i.e., The distance from C to C under the letter Aleph between the first and second partial is a perfect octave (P8). From the second to third partial, it's a perfect fifth and so on.) Note that as the pitches ascend, the intervals are closer together. Continuing up the harmonic series (it goes to infinity), the intervals become smaller (closer together). Eventually, every note of the musical scale shows up in the harmonic series. As previously noted, the first four partials are the most prominent.

First 9 letters of Hebrew alphabet with their musical frequencies and harmonics of fundamental note

Series: C	1	2 (P8)	3 (P5)	4 (P4)	5 (M3)	6 (m3)	7 (m3)	8 (M2)	9 (M2)	10 (M2)
Aleph	C	C	G	C	E	G	Bb	C	D	E
Bet	C	C	G	C	E	G	Bb	C	D	E
Gimel	G	G	D	G	B	D	F	G	A	B
Dalet	C	C	G	C	E	G	Bb	C	D	E
He	E	E	B	E	G#	B	D	E	F#	G#
Vav	G	G	D	G	B	D	F	G	A	B
Zayin	Bb	Bb	F	Bb	D	F	Ab	Bb	C	D
Chet	C	C	G	C	E	G	Bb	C	D	E
Tet	D	D	A	D	F#	A	C	D	E	F#

Figure 7

In this chart (Figure 7), the first (fundamental note) is the key signature for a specific Hebrew letter. For example, the letter Zayin is represented by the fundamental pitch of B-flat. Therefore, the notes used when focusing on the letter Zayin will be in the key (mode) of B-flat. The first four notes (Bb to Bb: an octave higher, F: a P5 higher, and Bb: a P4 higher yet) are the foundational notes in the harmonic structure of a melody.

Keep in mind that two more harmonic series are represented by the remaining Hebrew letters. When giving the final letters their own numeric value, there are twenty-seven total letters in the aleph-bet. Each harmonic series includes nine letters (9 x 3 = 27). Therefore, all twenty-seven letters of the Hebrew aleph-bet are used in this system. The twenty-seventh letter ends on the note C, which takes us back to the very beginning. It's circular, which lines up perfectly with the Hebraic monthly cycle. We now begin to see how all the pieces fit together.

Healing in the Hebrew Months and Musical Frequencies in the Aleph-bet

In this section, we look at each Hebrew month, the Hebrew letter for that month, and the musical note for the letter. Ian Clayton, a businessman, coined the term "bench of three," which represents a governmental authority. For example, earthly government in many countries often operates with three branches: judicial, legislative, and executive. All three are needed to run the government.

Musically speaking, three notes create a chord (major, minor, diminished, etc.). The Trinity is another bench of three (Father, Son, and Holy Spirit). Here, we have another bench of three: Hebrew months, a musical frequency, and a Hebrew letter. I can't help but wonder how this bench of three works. I believe it's multi-dimensional as we'll see in the descriptions.

Each of the Hebrew months is listed in order, starting from Nisan. The corresponding Hebrew letter and musical frequency are listed at the beginning. Although I don't go into detail in this book, these descriptions are part of the Song of the Month activations. I focus on the protocol of how we stay in good health set within the Hebraic calendar. This is a quick synopsis to assist those on a journey into wholeness by focusing on how an ancient culture used a monthly cycle to stay healthy – spirit, soul, and body. Whatever your personal beliefs may be, consider that this information is an ancient tradition still used today. That alone says there's something to it.

For the Song of the Month, I create a spontaneous instrumental piece of music based on the fundamental frequency of the note for that month. The activation (voice-over activation) walks the listener through what properties of that month I sense the listener should focus on. Yes, this changes from year to year because we change. Things in our world system can dictate how we look at our personal lives. Therefore, the focus often changes to assist people through those situations from year to year.[xxv]

Every month has a theme. Within that theme are several variations. The variation played out is often personal in nature. A variation might have many levels (dimensions). This process becomes multi-dimensional, just like we are multi-dimensional and complicated beings. Therefore, the process can never remain the same for every month of every year. When I create a new song and activation each month for my subscribers, it changes from year to year.

At the end of each month's description below, I provide an activation. The purpose of the activation is to apply the properties of the month and Hebrew letter to assist on your journey into wholeness—spirit, soul, and body. Each month has a special focus. Ideas from these activations go into my Song of the Month where I aurally and musically walk people through it. It does change from year to year as previously mentioned. As I grow and mature, I receive more revelation about each month and letter. I then pass that along to the Song of the Month subscribers in their monthly subscription. What's in this book will more than likely grow and expand as I continue this journey. https://www.healingfrequenciesmusic.com/product-category/song-of-the-month/

Throughout each month, I mention the musical note and that you might consider playing music in the "key signature" of that note. The key signature includes modes, minor keys, major keys, or music with a drone. At the time of this writing (September 2019), I'm working on creating three additional albums that concentrate on each letter of the Hebrew aleph-bet to assist those on this journey. Each album focuses on the nine notes in the three harmonic series with special attention to the meaning of each letter. I hope to have them completed by January 2022. When those albums are available, you'll find them under the "Shop" tab on the Healing Frequencies Music website.[xxvi]

You will find some keys as you work through this. The first is consistency. This requires patience and perseverance. We cannot work on wholeness without some form of consistency. The hit-and-miss approach generally doesn't serve us well. Find a daily time, even if it's for ten minutes, and do some form of the activations. Pick one or two points on the activation list for each month. Choose what resonates with you this year. As you go through the cycle from year to year, different activations may pop out as if to be saying, "pick me!" Whatever you choose, be consistent if you want lasting results.

Here are some additional tips:

- Put on some calming instrumental music. The lyrics in music with words gives direction. Instrumental music allows the focus to be on the activation not on the words in a song. However, if a specific song is speaking to you on a given day and you feel it's perfect for the activation, use it. If you have no direction, I generally recommend instrumental music. If you need some instrumental music, I have plenty to choose from on the Healing Frequencies Music website.

- All the months have a musical note associated with them. Look for music that focuses on that note. I won't repeat this information each month, so add this to your monthly to-do list. It brings another dimension (or layer) into the recipe.

- Grab a journal and write what comes to mind. The activations foster a time of intimacy with God. You'll sense, see, hear, and feel things that may not make sense. Write them down to consider later. As you read journal entries many months later, you'll be amazed at how what didn't make sense begins to gel for you. Journaling is important for a reason.

- As you engage with God through these activations, you may learn that some things are holding you back. Unforgiveness puts the brakes on forward motion. If you feel stuck, look to see if unforgiveness may have you sitting at a stop sign. Let go, give it to God, and trade it for something that fosters good health. You may sense, see, hear, or feel methods of doing this.

- Create decrees and declarations that bring you into wholeness and health. Use the information from each month to decree and declare over your own situation. Find out what God says about that situation and make your decrees accordingly. Remember, thoughts, intents, and words create a frequency. Negative words create lower frequencies that put our bodies at risk for illness. Helpful, positive, and the-glass-is-half-full thoughts, intents, and words create a higher frequency, which then allows our bodies to naturally heal. Life and death are controlled through the power of the tongue. (See Proverbs 18:21.)

- Ponder on the activations throughout the day. Be proactive by taking the bull by the horns and not fearing the process. Ponderings often lead to answers that come from the strangest places. God speaks to us all day long. How are we listening for his voice? During times of pondering and meditation we can gain some of the best insight. Meditation in this sense is about focusing on one thing: God. Build intimacy with him like you do with a best friend.

- This is a process. It takes time so don't beat yourself up when you miss it. Get back up when you fall and continue the journey.

- Your imagination is from God. If this worries you, sanctify your imagination before starting the activations. At times, the first thoughts, images, and feelings are from God, but we blow them off. We say, "That must have been the pizza I ate last night!" We first engage God through our imagination. See yourself with him in a favorite place and having a conversation with him as you do the activations. This, too, takes practice.

- Practice, practice, practice! If you miss a day or two, it's no big deal. But practice being consistent. This, too, takes time. Forming new habits requires consistency. The more you do something, the quicker it becomes a part of you

- Join the Healing in the Hebrew Months Facebook group to find community with others on this journey www.facebook.com/groups/healinginthehebrew months

Nisan ניסן

Starts in March or April
Letter: *Heh* ה
Musical Note: *E*

Nisan is the first month of the Jewish New Year. The holiday of Passover is celebrated during the month of Nisan from the 15th through the 22nd. Passover commemorates the Jewish people's miraculous redemption from slavery in Egypt and the birth of the Jewish nation.

God pulled his people out of Egyptian slavery and began the attempt to get them into the promised land. This is pivotal in journeying out of bondage. Nisan can mean "miracles," "to move," or "to start." It is often referred to as "the month of redemption." According to the sages, "In Nisan our forefathers were redeemed from Egypt and in Nisan we will be redeemed."[xxvii]

In Nisan, we declare ourselves free in any areas where we've felt enslaved so that we can move migrate out of our "personal Egypt." It's a new beginning for each new year and a place to start fresh. This is a great month to take a word or phrase and declare that over ourselves throughout the entire year. This will bring lasting inner change.

Nisan is also associated with our voice. Just as God created the world with his voice, we create as well. We can only experience freedom when we walk out of slavery. Leave Egypt behind! During Nisan, we learn to step out into the unknown. We declare ourselves free to move forward. This month, we set our focus on our thoughts, intents, words, and actions. We see the creative power of positive words override the negative. Nisan is the time to start speaking positively over our circumstances.

The letter *Heh* has a gematria of five. It's a picture of a man with arms raised as if to say, "Lo! Behold!" Other definitions include: see, behold (therefore), breath, a lattice or window for the purpose of seeing. The musical note is E. Heh also represents the garments of thought, speech, and action with five elements. Two are levels of thought (imagination and meditation). The next are two levels of speech that include the words of the heart and the words of the mouth. The final level is action, which totals five levels. The gematria of five ties nicely with these five levels.[xxviii]

As we go through the month of Nisan, we connect the letter Heh with the month. The musical note is E. It's as if we're saying, "Lo and behold! My deliverance is at hand! I am moving into my promised land." We declare ourselves free from what enslaved us in the past season. Rabbi Raskin suggests concrete actions: watch our thoughts, speech, and actions. These create a bench of three to bring a governmental authority into our lives. When we use our imagination to meditate on God's perspective through situations in our lives, our focus is on the solution, not the problem.[xxix]

Nisan Activation

1. Define your personal Egypt and write it down. If more than one thing comes to mind, write them all down.

2. Are you in bondage to anything? If so, write them down.

3. See yourself hand those things over to God and trade them for the opposite thing. For example, if you fear financial lack, what does the opposite trade look like? God will show you. If several items are on your list, take an item per day and partner with God for a solution.

4. Write out some decrees and declarations that help you step into the unknown and begin saying them consistently over yourself.

5. Focus on thoughts, intents, and speech throughout this month. Take an inventory of what needs to be changed in this area and make declarations and decrees that foster the desired thoughts, intents, and words.

6. Spend some time worshipping. This always helps put negative stuff in its proper place: at the feet of Jesus. Consider choosing music in the key of E since that's the musical pitch for the letter Heh.

On the Healing Frequencies Music website, under the sample page, I list all the fundamental notes used for each song. The free download, "Beloved Friend," is also in the key of E.

7. Step into the center of the letter Heh. What does it feel like to be in that place – the picture of a man with his arms raised? See yourself in that position throughout this month partnering with God through Heh. Worship! Lo and behold, your deliverance has come!

   See yourself walking out of the past season and into the new through worship, joy, and gladness.

   Move into the promised land daily. Imagine the movement with your imagination (spiritual eyes) as you take daily steps forward into the promises.

   Practice looking forward as you stay in that attitude of worship.

Iyar אייר

Starts in April or May
Letter: *Vav* ו
Musical Note: *G*

Iyar is the second month on the Jewish calendar after Nisan. “Shortly after the Exodus, the thirsty Israelites reached a well of bitter water. Moses cast a tree into the water, and it miraculously became sweet. G-d then promised that if Israel followed His ways, ‘the diseases I have placed on Egypt I will not place upon you, for I am G-d your Healer (אני י-י רפאך).’ The acronym for this last phrase spells out the name of the month of Iyar (אייר), thus indicating that Iyar is a propitious time for healing.”[xxx]

In Nisan, we walk out of captivity, leaving the slave mentality. As negative issues came up during Passover, we will work through these areas in the next five months. At times, we must walk out some things, much like the Israelites had to spend time in the desert to work through the issues that held them back. Fear of the unknown was a big one for them.

In Iyar, we develop greater sensitivity to hear Holy Spirit, to be in tune and in timing with God, and to understand his secrets. We should consider physical as well as emotional healing. We also need to look at where bitterness resides in our lives and allow the sweetness of God to come in.

God taught a lesson using bitter water in the well by saying, “This isn’t just about fixing water. If you listen to me, you won’t have any of the diseases that the Egyptians have, for I am Jehovah Rapha, God your Healer.” Iyar is an acronym for “I am God Your Healer” in Hebrew. This is preventative language here. So often, our internal bitterness is the result of our focus. We can choose to see the good in a situation, or we can stew and complain. A good way to work around this is by recounting what God has done for us during the day.[xxxi]

Iyar is a month to really focus on what comes out of our mouth. What we say creates a frequency. Negative speech/thoughts create a low frequency which opens us up to illness. Positive speech and thoughts help us vibrate at a higher frequency, which keeps us healthier overall. Scientific studies are beginning to demonstrate the importance of our thoughts, words, and actions. If we want to stay healthy, the first place to start is with the flapping of the lips. To control that, we must reframe our thoughts and intents because out of the mouth comes what's truly in our hearts. (See Luke 6:45.) In other words, out of what's deep within the heart, the mouth utters.

Yes, truth is behind a "Pollyanna" attitude. Playing the "glad game" the way the character Pollyanna did in the movie might benefit us in more ways than we can imagine. If you've never seen the movie, consider checking it out.

The letter *Vav* transforms the past into the future. It's also "wherefore or therefore" that represents a holding together of something or connecting piece. The original pictograph was a hook or tent peg. A hook also holds two things together. Here, it's a connection of the spiritual and physical. As we engage the letter Vav, we can connect directly to God. The gematria is six, which indicates completion. It also represents all six sides: north, south, west, east, above, and below. The musical note is G. Choosing music in the key of G is another part of the recipe within the dimensional layers of Iyar.[xxxii]

Iyar Activation

1. Iyar is a continuation of Nisan. It's the second month in five-month process. As negative issues come up, take the opportunity to declare ourselves free.

2. Iyar is a "month on the move," where we begin the process of moving into the promised land. See yourself taking those forward steps so you're not looking back like Lot's wife did. When we constantly turn around and look at the past, we've stopped any forward movement. Make decrees to assist in looking ahead.

3. As with the month of Nisan, take an inventory of what comes out of your mouth. When it's negative, trade it for the positive and decree that over yourself.

4. Find a quiet place daily. Listen to music if it helps bring calm and peacefulness to your being. Meditate on the goodness of God and see him help you walk away from your personal Egypt and into the promised land. At first, this is by faith, especially if we're not well-versed in using our imaginations. Keep practicing! You'll get there.

5. The goal is to transform the past into the future through the assistance of the Father, Son, and Holy Spirit. As you build this relationship, journal what you see, sense, hear, and feel.

6. See yourself as the authority over the "mountain" of your life with you on top "in Christ." Our strength is in him. When we invite him into that place of rest and peace, our relationship with him becomes the focal point, and the circumstances take a back seat. We learn to view the circumstances through his eyes, which are often different from our world view. This is a huge focus for Iyar because in that place of rest and peace, we are on the top of our mountain with Christ.

7. Begin to focus on any physical issues. Write out declarations and decrees that help you see wholeness in your physical body. Speak these out on the top of the mountain of your life as Jesus stands with you in agreement. Visualize a mountain. See Jesus there with you. If you get pictures of what this mountain looks like, write it down. That will come into play later.

8. The letter Vav is associated with Iyar. As a tent peg, Vav holds things firmly. Stand next to the letter (in your imagination) and feel the strength of such a small tool that can hold down a large tent. See it as a foundation, a holding place, and a place of security.

The letter Vav is a transformation letter, just like Iyar is a transformation month. From that holding place, see yourself stepping out, continuing to move forward into your promised land. This is the reason that the words of our mouth are so important. Vav helps us be firm and in position. We can do that with our words and actions.

Think of that holding place of steadfastness, like a tent peg, as you move through the month of Iyar. Make declarations over your forward movement while standing next to Vav throughout the month.

Sivan סיון

Starts in May or June
Letter: *Zayin* ז
Musical Note: *B-flat*

Sivan is the third month on the Jewish calendar after Nisan. *Rosh Chodesh Sivan* is distinguished as the day the Jewish people arrived and camped before Mount Sinai. "The Torah describes this with the phrase 'Israel camped before the mountain' (Exodus 19:2), where the verb *vayichan* ("camped") is stated in a singular form, in contrast to the other verbs in the narrative. This describes how the entire people camped 'as one person, with one heart,' expressing true unity."[xxxiii]

The month of Sivan is about both inheritance and new revelation. The two "arc" together to create an energy of expectation. As we address issues, we begin walking out what we declared during Nisan and Iyar. Remember—we declared ourselves free of bondage. That may look different for each person.

During this time, we meet with God for further instruction on the mountain of our life. We see this mountain through the eyes of our imagination where we can "survey" the situations in our life.

Shavout is the anniversary of when God gave the Jews the Torah at Mt. Sinai. This is when Judaism was born and when the covenant between God and his people was established. God acknowledged that even though all the nations were his, these people were set apart to be "a kingdom of priests and a holy nation."[xxxiv] Pentecost is the date of the new covenant when the people received the Holy Spirit and the Christian church was born. This appears to be a marked time for us to receive what God has for us. In both cases (Shavout and Pentecost), there's a time of waiting—waiting to receive from God.

Moses went up the mountain alone to meet with God. Other people around us might not be able to go where we are going. Much like God did with the Israelites, he makes personal covenants with us regarding our own life call. We have a personal mountain—a place of meeting with God.

Sivan is the arrival at our personal Mount Sinai, our personal mountain. We focus on encouragement, strength, and empowerment during this change. It's also time to receive a double portion of fruit and invite Wisdom to be with us in the journey. Notice a theme with several variations is playing out here. In music, we call that "theme and variations." Our theme here starts in the month of Nisan—the beginning of the new year when we walk out of our personal Egypt, leaving behind old mindsets and junk we no longer need. Every year when we do this, any old baggage should be taken to the dump. The variation looks different each year because our circumstances change. During the month of Sivan, get on a steppingstone, even if you don't know what lies ahead! If fear tries to rear its ugly head, take the opportunity to look the other way into encouragement, strength, and empowerment. Our focus often dictates how we deal with the results.

Frank Sinatra sang the song "My Way." But the problem with doing things in our own strength is the inner conflict that holds us back. When we invite God and Wisdom to be with us on that journey, we can see another way—a way we often don't realize is there because of the blinders that cover our eyes. Humanistic thinking focuses on self. That may work for a season, but we truly need others to help us see what holds us back that we can't—or won't—see. That's one reason the Israelites worked as a group: to hold each other accountable.

The Hebrew letter for the month of Sivan is *Zayin*. Its gematria is seven. The original pictograph looks like a plow. It's also a mattock, a sharp pickax. This refers to food, cutting, and nourishment. Zayin can also mean "to arm or ornament." It speaks of abundance and fullness in brightness and full light. It can also be a doorpost, a holding device that gives stability. The word Zayin means "crown" or "weapon." Although the two words don't appear to relate, through the crown of creation, we have the weapon to overcome all negativity. Remember, on the seventh day, God sat back and rested in creation. The gematria of seven refers to God's rest on the seventh day. The musical note for the letter Zayin is B-flat.[xxxv]

Sivan Activation

1. Go back to your personal Mount Sinai. See yourself with the Trinity. Jesus is your advocate. Grab a journal and be prepared to write.

2. In Nisan and Iyar, you began walking out of your personal Egypt. Now it's a time to rest for a bit. In that place with the Trinity on your mountain, receive your double portion. Invite Wisdom to join you on the journey.

3. See yourself in the Light of God in all his fullness. Fill up with all that God is so you're well-nourished for the continued journey. Think of it as packing for a camping trip and preparing all the supplies needed for that trip. Do this "in the spirit" through the sanctified imagination with the Trinity. They'll help you know what to pack and how to pack it. Write it all down so you remember what tools you have brought with you.

4. Focus on overcoming negativity and continue ridding yourself of any negative thought process that holds you back.

5. Spend some time in that place of rest. A good way to do this is put on music in the key of B-

flat. This note is paired with Zayin and Sivan. See yourself entraining to the frequency of God. This aligns your thoughts with His. Receive nourishment during this time. How that looks and feels will differ for each person.

6. Create an energy of expectation through the letter Zayin. See abundance and light as you stand near it. After Moses went up the mountain to meet with God, he came down so full of light that the people could hardly look upon his face. Zayin is also full of nourishment needed for your continual journey as you, too, go up your mountain to meet with God. Do this daily to receive the needed spiritual nourishment for the month. See yourself marinate in the light and Glory of God. Let them permeate through your being.

7. Practice, practice, practice! The more you do it, the more adept you become at using your imagination as a gateway into the realms of the kingdom of heaven where the Trinity dwells. Go to them through the gateway of your personal mountain. When we're in Christ and he's in us, we are in that place of rest. We're then in position to receive our double portion so we can walk it out. This is the needed steppingstone to move forward.

Tammuz תמוז

Starts in June or July

Letter: ***Chet*** **ח**

Musical Note: ***C***

Tammuz is the fourth of the twelve months of the Jewish calendar. The month of Tammuz begins the season of the summer (Tammuz, *Av*, and *Elul*). The 17th day of Tammuz marks the beginning of a period known as the Three Weeks. This is an annual mourning period when the Jews mourn the destruction of the Holy Temple. It reaches a climax and concludes with the fast of the Ninth of Av, the date when both Holy Temples were set aflame.

> G-d is our Father, and we are His children. During *galut* (exile), we constitute a dysfunctional family. We have been expelled from our Father's home, and our relationship is strained. This is certainly not the way the relationship should be—and this wasn't

> always the case. There was a time when we were coddled by our Father's embrace. His love for us manifested itself in many forms, including miracles, prophets, abundant blessings, and a land flowing with milk and honey. At the center of our relationship was the Holy Temple, G-d's home, where He literally dwelt among His people and where His presence was tangible.[xxxvi]

Tammuz marks the beginning of a pondering season. During this time, read through journals, review dreams, and any other spiritual documentation. Are there connecting pieces or patterns? Is there a step of faith to take at this time? Let's not forget our Source. Take this time to focus on looking forward and resist falling back into old belief systems. This is a month of choices.

> As a reminder, Moses went up the mountain on the 7th of Sivan to receive the Torah. He had to spend the next 40 days up there getting the full revelation. The people waited, and due to a miscommunication, thought he was supposed to be back on the 16th of Tammuz. When he wasn't, panic set in that they were suddenly leaderless, and Moses probably burned to a crisp up there, or as the Talmud put it, 'Satan showed them Moses, dead lying on a bier.' Their journey had been fueled by Moses' inspiration, vision and the miracles he brought about. Without their leader they felt doomed to die in the desert.

> In short, they defaulted to what they were comfortable with in the crisis.[xxxvii]

We might want to ask ourselves what our triggers are when life gets tough. What kind of actions do we take when we lose trust in God? "On the 17th of Tammuz, there should be an ultimate paradigm shift and clear route to our 'promised land' because that was when the golden calf of idolatry was smashed into bits. Various patterns of idolatry have followed on Tammuz's since. Does that mean we're in a bad month? Hardly! But it is a month of challenge, confrontation, and extremes, and not one where you can pick the middle of the road."[xxxviii]

The Hebrew letter for the month of Tammuz is *Chet* with a gematria of eight. The pictograph resembles a ladder if standing up or a tent wall on its side. The musical note is C. Chet is a marriage of two letters, Zayin and Vav. One represents the female, and the other, male. The joining of two important pieces brings unity. Chet also means "outside, divide, half, fence, an enclosure or something fenced in." It's also a place of refuge, much like Noah's ark was for the people and animals during the flood. The number eight can represent transcendence, a level beyond nature and intellect and a level beyond the natural order as represented by the number seven.[xxxix]

Tammuz Activation

1. From your personal mountain, begin to have conversations with the Trinity concerning prophetic words, dreams, and visions you've had over time.

   See what these all mean from their perspective. Consider spending the entire month in reflection, taking the needed time to understand what you've received at a deeper level.

2. As before, this is from a position of rest. We use the phrase "come up here" as John described in a vision in Revelation 4:1. This is a higher realm where the situations on earth are at a lower level or "under our feet." (See Romans 16:20.)

   We look directly into the face of Jesus and entrain with his frequency until we sense peace. We then meditate on functioning out of that place of rest in Christ.

3. This is a month to practice trusting in our Source—the one true and living God—YHVH. This can only come from a position of rest in Christ. This is an aspect of the letter Chet where we go for answers beyond our nature and intellect. We go directly to the Source from that

position of rest.

4. The goal this month is simple because we're continuing to walk out that five months of leaving negativity behind. Continue to keep negativity in check.

5. We've packed necessary provisions for our journey in Sivan. Along with taking an inventory of our prophetic words, revelations, and visions, ask God to show us how our necessary provisions fit into our journey forward.

6. The letter Chet looks like a ladder standing up or a wall on its side. As a "living letter," what could this represent for you? Imagine that you're standing on the ladder or sitting on the fence. Consider the ladder position as taking a step of faith into the mysteries of God. These are mysteries specifically for you to discover on your journey this year.

   The ladder also leads into that place of transcendence. As a fence, see Chet as a place of refuge. Throughout Tammuz, sit on the fence and get on the ladder with Chet. Step into the mysteries and refuge that God has for you. Marinate in the mysteries so when they're unveiled, you'll already be resonating in the frequency that they carry.

Av אב

Starts in July or August

Letter: *Tet* ט

Musical Note: *Av*

The name of the eleventh [fifth][xl] month on the Jewish calendar, Av, literally means "father." It is customary to add the name "Menachem," which means "comforter" or "consoler"—so Menachem Av. In this month, both Temples were destroyed, and many other tragedies occurred. Yet our Father in heaven is there to comfort and console us. Av is a "low point" on the Jewish calendar—the Ninth of Av, the day of the sin of the spies, and the destruction of both the First and Second Temples in Jerusalem. But it also incorporates a "high point": the 15th of Av, a day designated for finding one's predestined soulmate, and one of the happiest days on the Jewish calendar.[xli]

The month of Av might seem conflicted with itself as you have both low and high points, which may feel a bit chaotic. Most of us know the feeling of chaos. During Av, we should realize that we are more than capable and that if we push through, we will find solutions. We can focus on a fully functioning intuition so that our spiritual senses work better. We can look at resources that could be missing so we can seize the moment. If we resolve to be unstoppable, then doubts easily float by us. During the tough times, we need to stay close to those who encourage us. If none of those people are around, this may be a bit more difficult but not impossible. Where there's a will, there's a way.

Even in that low place, you need to focus on the light at the end of the tunnel during Av. Make a choice to look past the circumstances. During any trial, just like I mentioned previously about Pollyanna, you can still make choices about what to look at and focus on.

As I mentioned in the first paragraph, Av represents father, comforter, and consoler. When circumstances aren't going well, we still look to the Source. The problem with looking within is that during inner conflict, we bring that conflict to our viewing window. We must get outside ourselves in order to see how G-d can use any difficulty to help us grow and mature. Av is the opportunity to take any situation, especially the hard ones, to ask "How can I grow in this?"

During the month of Av (5778 or the year 2018), the whole eminent domain process for our entire neighborhood kicked into high gear. No one wants to lose their home to a highway project, so we had a choice to make. Would we grumble and complain about the situation or look to see what good could come from it? Obviously, I chose the latter, and as a result, I have a home that I love even more than the home I lost. The journey was far from easy but that's only because of how I chose to look at the situation.

Some low points may not actually occur in the month of Av. But low points are probably on either side of it. Take this time to choose what to look at during the situation. Let our spiritual senses work at their peak. Seize the moment, resolve to be unstoppable, and let those doubts pass on by. Character is built during the tough times. It's time to let the trials and circumstances of life "make us instead of break us."

The letter *Tet* is associated with Av. The original pictograph was a basket. The gematria is nine. The musical note is D. Tet means "good or best." A basket implies something that's knit together, interwoven and twisted. It's a place of surrounding that contains something. Weaving creates a vortex or spiral. The number nine corresponds to the months of pregnancy. It's considered a "true" number from the beginning, middle, and end as represented in the three letters of the word: aleph, mem, tav. The lesson is that what is true resonates from the beginning to the middle and finally through the end.[xlii]

Av Activation

1. Av is the fourth month of putting negativity in check. Give it a ticket and send it packing. It's a continual process of developing the habit of releasing the opposite into our being so we function in a higher frequency, which brings us into better health.

2. We've gathered resources in Sivan and Tammuz for a journey. In Av, we focus on developing a higher level of intuition as we're seated in Christ. In Tammuz, we took inventory by looking at our prophetic words, dreams, and visions. In Christ, we gain greater revelation into how those play out in our lives. This leads to greater intuition in general, which takes practice.

3. We're still on the journey into our personal promised land. We now have provision and tools necessary for that journey. In Av, we begin to see how those tools are used.

4. Circumstances arise along the way and as they do, ask "How can I grow in this?"

5. In the letter Tet, we see God's "good or best" in any situation. We see his truth from the beginning to the middle then to the end. We do

this from the position of being in Christ, which is the necessary relational aspect to take the chaos out of a journey.

6. Step inside the basket of the letter Tet. Use your imagination to see yourself in that place of protection where God has you surrounded by his love. Ponder and meditate on the "good or best" while in this position of protection.

   When life throws curve balls at you, go to this place of rest. See yourself "in" Christ, just like an item is placed "in" a basket. Av is a month to focus on how we respond to chaos that's around us. The picture that we're given this month of the basket provides a visual of the "in Christ" principle. Consider this your invitation to step in.

Elul אלול

Starts in August or September

Letter: *Yod* י

Musical Note: *C*

Elul is the twelfth [sixth][xliii] and final month in the Jewish calendar. This month connects the past year with the coming year, a time when we reflect on where we stand and where we should be going. Elul is a month of repentance, mercy, and forgiveness.

> In Tammuz, the Jews sinned with the golden calf; on Rosh Chodesh Elul, Moses ascended to Mount Sinai for a third 40-day period until Yom Kippur, when he descended with the second tablets (luchot) and G-d's word of joyful, wholehearted forgiveness. (The first time Moses ascended was to receive the first tablets; the second time was after the sin, to ask for forgiveness; and this third time was to receive the second set of tablets.) These were

> days when G-d revealed to the Jewish people great mercy. Since then, this time has been designated as a time of mercy and forgiveness, an opportune time for teshuvah—repentance.[xliv]

The four letters of the name Elul are an acronym for the phrase in Song of Songs 6:3: "I am to my beloved and my beloved is to me" (author's paraphrase). During Elul, we enjoy God's presence when we can focus on healing from relational issues. During Elul, God's closeness to us is most easily felt and/or perceived. It is as though an invisible curtain that we ourselves designed via poor judgements, fear and pain, is drawn aside. God meets us where we are. Jewish texts refer to this time as "the King is in the field."

> The parable is that for the most of the year, the King is in a palace, and to see or speak with him, you have to journey there, dress right, talk right, jump through all the hoops, and even then, only a select few get in. But there were times when the king would go out among the people and set up a tent in a field where he was accessible to all. Anyone could go, as they are, and be received. At the end, the people escort the king back to the palace but this time they are not shut out. Through relationship built in the field, they now have access to the throne. As you know, we have access via Jesus, whenever, wherever, the King met us once and for all where we are.

> However, the season stands as one of intimacy and restoration.[xlv]

We can use the month of Elul to strengthen connections to God and to each other. Mend fences and make things right with God and those around us. When our buttons are pushed, we have an opportunity to head for healing if we choose to see it that way. It truly is about letting our circumstances bring us into maturity. In addition, we can receive strategy, answers, and insight just as Moses did when he went to see God. He learned all about God's mercy and obtained his forgiveness and reconciliation with the people. We can follow suit in our own repentance.

It's also time to develop our visions, prayers, and hopes for yet another new year. The Hebrew year has lots of beginnings, and we're at another one. Had I not looked at the eminent domain situation as an opportunity to see how God was bringing me into a better place, my situation would be different now. Av and Elul involved checking out the buttons that pushed me so I could deal with them.

The letter *Yod* is associated with Elul. The original pictograph is an arm with an open hand. The musical note is E. The meaning of the word Yod is "Jew." This depicts God bringing the Israelites out of Egypt with a mighty hand. The outstretched hand of Yod indicates that something is held. Power and might fall into one's hand. With our hand, we can also make a fist. We work and worship with our hands. At times, we also give a blow or strike (pierce) with the hand. The number ten is a significant number for a Jew: ten commandments, ten plagues, ten utterances of speech (from the Sepher Yetzirah), ten generations from Adam to Noah and Noah to Abraham, etc. Ten represents sanctity and holiness and that God dwells in us.[xlvi]

Elul Activation

1. During Elul, we add more to the recipe—relationships with others. Begin to look at those relationships to see if any healing is needed.

2. This is the 5th and final month of focusing on rooting negativity out of our thoughts, intents, and words. We still consider this as the focus shifts to relational issues.

   How can relationships be mended? Should they be mended? Is divine subtraction in order? If so, is it for a season until negativity from that relationship is rooted out and replaced with something more positive?

3. Take time to go back up your personal mountain and have conversations with the Trinity about your relationships. In our relationship with God, we learn how to have relationships with others.

4. In that place of rest, marinate in God's mercy and forgiveness. The more we marinate in God's love, the more we understand our position in him. This helps our relationships with others.

5. Bring back that list of dreams, visions, and prophetic words. Put those before God and present them to him through sanctity and holiness.

6. Prepare for another new year where the outstretched hand of the Yod provides more tools for the journey. Power and might fall into your hands as you engage with the letter Yod in that place of rest in God. Worship and see yourself in God's outstretched hand.

7. The letter Yod is the first letter of God's name – YHVH (Yod, Heh, Vav, Heh). With hands reaching toward God, we entangle ourselves with all that he is. Elul is a month to build intimacy with God. This is demonstrated through the pictograph of an extended hand reaching out.

   Stand with Yod in that position of worship. The number ten often represents God dwelling with us in holiness. Imagine taking the place of the priest (since we are priests) in the Holy of Holies and begin to worship with all your might.

   Sing the name of God – YHVH. In that position, be filled and entangled with all that he is. This is a great exercise to do on a regular basis!

Tishrei תשרי

Starts in September or October

Letter: *Lamed* ל
Musical Note: *B*

Tishrei is full of meaningful days of celebration: High Holidays, Rosh Hashanah, the Ten Days of Repentance, Yom Kippur, *Sukkot*, and *Simchat Torah*. Each one has its own significant customs and rituals. Some are serious, set aside for reflection and soul-searching. Others are joyous, full of happy and cheerful celebration. The whole month provides opportunities to connect, be inspired, and become more fulfilled and in tune with our true inner selves. Tishrei is considered the head of the year, and the reservoir from which we draw our strength and inspiration throughout the year ahead.[xlvii]

Tishrei is the seventh month in the cycle and the Jewish new year. Nisan is the first month, and

Tishrei marks the beginning of a numerical change in date (e.g., 5778, 5779, etc.). There's a completion and beginning at the same time.

Rosh Hashanah lasts three days, starting at sundown the first day and ending at nightfall on the third day. One of the most significant observations of the holiday is the sounding of the Shofar. A total of one hundred notes are sounded each day. Tishrei is a time for reflection and review. The sound of a trumpet (shofar) symbolizes a message or word given, so look for new revelation this month.

Tishrei is a month to take an inventory of our talents. What are we naturally good at? Is there anything we don't have to work super hard at doing? Are there things we love that we haven't been able to do? Even if someone else doesn't think it's a talent and we do, we can still add that to the inventory. We live in our own skin—not someone else's. Take this month to journal and look through previous writings. It's like taking an inventory of our lives, or if we do this yearly, of everything in the past year. If some words still seem far off, they continue to be brought back each year. If you need some help with inventory, consider taking the Discovery Class in Dream Ventures. Everything in the Hebraic year is all about identity. This class is great for discovering our identity.[xlviii]

What is the purpose of all this? When we feel comfortable in our own skin, with who we are, and with who we're created to be, it's much easier to move forward in life. By now in this cycle, it's obvious that we first deal with inner issues. Very little is mentioned about physical health in this process. The Jewish culture practiced keeping their emotional lives healthy, so the physical was possibly easier to deal with. As we focus on our emotional well-being, the physical has a greater opportunity to come into line. The spirit comes first for a reason—then the soul, then the body. Ruling our lives from the spirit first provides a trickle-down effect. Ponder on this through the month of Tishrei.

Lamed is the letter of Tishrei. The original pictograph is a staff, much like a shepherd's rod. The gematria for Lamed is thirty. The musical note is B. Lamed means to "learn and teach." Through teaching and learning, we move toward, into, unto, even to, and beside certain goals. It's a connecting piece through the process of learning. The number 30 represents a fullness of strength. For the Jew, it's a new level of maturity. The power to begin transforming the world beings when a Jew reaches the age of thirty. Training leads to this transformation. The shepherd used his rod to keep the flocks out of danger. God helps keep us from harm during our maturing process if we allow him to.[xlix]

Tishrei Activation

1. This is a month of celebration and the head of the Jewish New Year. Get into party mode through extravagant worship in the presence of God. Be thankful for all the blessings received up to this point.

2. In a celebratory mode, go back to your personal mountain. From this place in Christ, take an inventory of your gifts and talents. You might see yourself sitting at a table with Jesus as if you're in a place of strategy. Ask and answer the questions (above) about your giftings. Strategize how they can be used in future seasons. Begin writing down ideas and discuss them with the Trinity.

3. Over the past few months, you've gathered tools for a journey. This is in preparation for the months of contemplation ahead. Prepare to go into that place of mystery and hiddenness so that like a caterpillar, you morph into something beautiful and new in the spring. On your personal mountain with Jesus, ask him to start showing you how to use those tools.

4. Look for new revelation throughout the month.

5. Take an inventory of your maturity level. Levels might differ in various parts of your life. In some areas, you're still learning, while in other areas, you have advanced to a teacher level. Ask God to show you the paths of learning and teaching in your life. What do you still need help in? What can you share with others to help them on their journeys?

6. Tishrei is a learning and teaching month. The pictograph for the corresponding letter, Lamed, is a staff. What's in a staff? Shepherd's lead flocks and point them in the right direction with a staff. Shepherds are "teachers" to their flocks.

   Using your imagination, stand next to the staff of Lamed. The gematria of 30 is paired with Lamed, indicating fullness and strength. Stand with the teacher in fullness and strength. See yourself resonate with all three to bring a three-stranded cord that's not easily broken into your life. It's a strong cord. When you add the musical frequency for this month into the mix (key of B), it adds another layer as a strong "chord."

Cheshvan חשון

Starts in October or November

Letter: ***Nun*** **נ**
Musical Note: ***A-flat***

Cheshvan is the eighth month of the Jewish calendar. Cheshvan is the only month with no holidays or special *mitzvot*.

During Cheshvan, the messiah is supposed to rebuild the temple. For those that believe Jesus is the messiah, the New Testament teaching says *we* are the temple, so that's a possible indication that a rebuilding may take place from the inside out. This lines up with Jewish thinking in general. Although Cheshvan may feel anti-climactic after all the celebration in Tishrei, we still need sustainable growth. During this same season, deciduous trees lose their leaves. They then enter a barren season where it appears as if nothing is happening. Some plants or crops, such as winter wheat, must go through what's called a vernalization process. During this time, the seed lays dormant (or so appears) to promote stronger growth in the actual growing season. Below the surface, roots grow deeper and stronger for the next season.[1]

If we look at Cheshvan as a transition month where there's a lull or even a sense of bleakness as preparation for what's coming up, we may fare better in the quick growth season. We need to embrace this transition, this lull, the bleakness. It's a time to prepare for the fruitfulness of the future.

Since we're dealing with roots, we can dig up root issues that are weeds in our lives before they go dormant in preparation for a spewing of nastiness in the spring. Anything in our past that creates an unhealthy mindset can potentially stunt healthy growth in the new season. Unhealthy roots are typically distortions of the way we see ourselves. If our identity is wrapped up in the unhealthy root, it will choke out what's supposed to come up in the future. This is a time to find what's unhealthy and dig it up. Since this is very much about our identity, we may also continue to challenge conclusions that we came to in early childhood about who we are. Just because someone said something to us as a child doesn't mean it's the truth. I had an eighth grade math teacher who told me I'd never amount to anything. That was a lie. It took me several years to step out of that lie and into the truth of who I was meant to be. When we live out of someone else's truth for us, we are living a lie.

As we take inventory of identity during Cheshvan, we can pull out any lingering bitter roots. We only want the healthy ones to grow. The roots that need that marinating time in preparation for the spring growth have the needed space to shoot up and say, "Here I am, world!"

Nun is the letter for Cheshvan. The original pictograph looks like a seed (representing life). The gematria for Nun is fifty. The musical note is A-flat. Nun has several meanings. Both "kingship" and "fish" fit quite nicely for the month of Cheshvan. As a seed, the pictograph represents an heir, a son, to sprout, put forth, or to propagate. As an heir, sons become kings. Kings bring forth more heirs that step into their positions of authority. The number fifty represents a year of jubilee. It also represents the fifty gates of understanding where an individual must partner with God on the fiftieth level of transcendence. It's all about relationship in and through this process.[li]

Cheshvan Activation

1. You've come out of a month of celebration. At times, it may feel a bit like a letdown. In those moments, step back into that place of rest and keep your eyes on Jesus.

2. There is still a celebration—the year of jubilee. Each year of your life represents a step toward jubilee. Rejoice in how far you've made it despite what situations might look like around you.

3. We are kings and priests. Marinate in that and see yourself as a king who has heirs. This is how we take inventory of our identity. We're seated in Christ with the full benefits of kingship. Bumpy roads along the way don't change our identity but build character and maturity. See God's truth for you instead of someone else's. Journal during this time.

4. As with previous months, continue developing a deeper relationship with God. This is often a season of growing deeper roots. It may seem like not much is happening but remember the wheat and deciduous trees. They need time to develop a strong root system, which they can do in this beginning season. Allow a deep-rooted

relationship with the Trinity to strengthen that bond.

5. The picture of Nun resembles a seed. Seeds grow and produce fruit. For a season, seeds are in a hidden place where no one can see them. Then, one day, they sprout from that dark place into the light. It's in the non-visible seasons where "grounding" occurs so a seed has the strength to push through darkness, muck and mire.

   Strength forms during our bleakest moments when we don't give up! See yourself as a seed during Cheshvan brewing up some yummy goodness that's about to spring forth.

   Focus on the good, the beautiful, and what's yet to come amid any dark moment throughout the month. This may also be a time where you see or sense "seeds" of ideas coming from up within you. Be sure to write it all down!

Kislev כסלו

Starts in November or December

Letter: *Samech* ס
Musical Note: *B*

Kislev is the ninth month on the Jewish calendar after Nisan. It is best known for the holiday of Chanukah, which begins on 25 Kislev. The message of Chanukah is the eternal power of light over darkness or good over evil. "Aside from commemorating the miraculous victory of the small Jewish army over the mighty Syrian-Greek empire, Chanukah celebrates the miracle of the oil. When the Jews sought to light the Temple menorah after the war, they found only one small jug of pure oil. Miraculously, the one-day supply burned for eight days, and the sages instituted the eight-day festival of Chanukah, on which we kindle the menorah nightly."[lii]

Dreams and visions (day or night) are a natural time when God often speaks to us. Consider your dreams and visions during Kislev. This is a season of shorter days and longer nights. Night is for discovering mysteries and seeing things not yet revealed. It's time to get night vision, to go into the deep places, and to come out the other side. It's not distance from God but of being in a place where we sense his presence on a different level than we have in the past. We may see him at work in our lives, but we walk in faith walk because we're in the place of mystery, waiting for revelation.

As we go through Kislev, take time to look at the mystery in the darkness to see what needs to be revealed. We need to find our light in the darkness, light what we have, and let the revealing begin. They key is to keep the darkness from negatively overwhelming us.

Samech is the letter for Kislev. The original pictograph was a hand on the staff, signifying support. The gematria is sixty. The musical pitch is B. The design of Samech represents a closed circle, which indicates infinity. The word "samech" is an acronym for "to forgive, to pardon, and to atone." The pictograph is also a thorn. We might seem to be in a time of pain where we grab onto the support and protection that we need amid harmful or even hateful situations. It's a time to hold onto God's love and strength. Our support is in God who sustains and upholds us. Placed in another position, samech is a ladder that connects the lower to the higher.[liii]

Kislev Activation

1. Of all the months so far, Kislev appears the darkest. The winter season seems darker in the natural. In those places of hiddenness, we can marinate in God's light, glory, and love.

   Let that bench of three permeate your being. From that position of rest, be infused with God's light, glory, and love. Allow the process of the cocoon to do its work in you in that place of hiddenness.

2. Practice viewing the night as a time for making discoveries—discoveries to be revealed in their proper timing. This is where we develop night vision and learn to put our trust and hope in God. It's a time of patience and continued deep rooting. Practice patience in situations that don't make sense.

3. See and decree the miraculous over your life.

4. Continue to be mindful of thoughts, intents, and words. Line them up with decrees that God shows you in those mysterious places.

5. Meditate on the mysteries of God, believing by faith that truth is revealed. Journal about the

mysteries and truths you receive during this time.

6. Samech reminds us that even though there's pain in our life, we can grab onto God for strength and protection. In the "closed circle" of Samech, we feel the infinite love of God. It's another marinating position in a closed space. His love sustains and holds us through infinity.

   Kislev is a month that's set to bring us out of darkness. See yourself in the infinite circle of Samech. Feel God's love as you allow the frequency of love to permeate your being. This is a preparation month so fill up! Fill up your gas tank with God's love so that it continually sustains and protects you. When your tank is near empty, get into that circle and refill!

Tevet טבת

Starts in December or January

Letter: *Ayin* ע
Musical Note: *D*

Tevet is the tenth month on the Jewish calendar, counting from Nisan. Its name, which is mentioned in the book of Esther, was acquired in Babylonia. Tevet begins with the last days of Chanukah. The 10th of Tevet is a day of fasting, commemorating the start of the siege of Jerusalem in the year 3336 (425 BCE), which led to the destruction of the first *Beit Hamikdash* (holy temple) two-and-a-half years later on the ninth of Av.

> On a fast day, the Divine attribute of mercy is able to be drawn down into this world. By fasting over the destruction of the Temple, one 'sweetens' G-d's anger with Israel, the cause of the destruction. Our sages explain, 'Every generation for which the Temple is not rebuilt, is as though the Temple was

> destroyed for that generation.' As such, a fast day is not really a sad day, but an opportune day. It's a day when we are empowered to fix the cause of that first destruction, so that our long exile will end, and we will find ourselves living in Messianic times.[liv]

It's easy to imagine the anger and frustration of the Jews over the destruction of the temple as well as the siege of Jerusalem. Tevet gets its name from Babylon. In Akkadian, the name is *Tabito* and refers to a sinking into (like mud). In Hebrew, Tevet is the word *tov*, meaning "good." When comparing these two definitions, our focus could go either direction. Tevet is an Ayin month (the letter associated with Tevet), and we're in an Ayin decade. The original pictograph of Ayin is an eye, which means to "look and look again."

Tevet is a time when we can see what we could not before. As we look and look again, we see what needs to be done. We see new strategies and new paths to freedom. With better vision, we mirror that with a need for the eyes of our understanding to be enlightened with the truth. From here, we look to see the best and the potential in others, our circumstances, and ourselves. When we do see evil, we release words of life directly into the evil. As we see past our anger, frustration, and judgment toward ourselves and toward other, we release life into evil.

We can easily be angry at God for where we are and what we continue to deal with. Our attitudes and words can bring life to even the most difficult circumstances. It's time to abandon any kind of victim mentality and realize we are not stuck and that we're not sinking in the mud. In what may seem like a sticky situation, we can make a choice as to how we react *to* that situation. As anger, victimization, frustration, and judgments surface, we need to stop and really look at what's going on. If we are having an issue with people, are those traits in some way a part of ourselves that we don't like? What we often hate in others, we're doing ourselves. (*Ouch*!)

Throughout Tevet, if we focus on looking deep within at what triggers anger and frustration, we can come out of the darkness and into the light so that true light, revealed in the darkness, can shine forth. Remember, this month is still a dark month so what comes out of Kislev is revealed in Tevet.

The gematria for the month of Tevet is seventy, and the musical pitch is D. With our eyes, we see, watch, and show expression. Through the expression of the eyes, we see knowledge and character. As our eyes are on God, we see the mouth of God speak. Ayin also refers to a spring or fountain, a form of cleansing and purification. The number 70 represents one who has walked through the seven general emotional characteristics. Each of these has ten levels for a total of seventy. At the age of seventy, those who walk close to God share their wisdom with others. They are masters of themselves, allowing them to teach others.[lv]

Tevet Activation

1. Consider a day of fasting as a form of empowerment over any destruction in your life. In Christ, we bring his grace and mercy into any destructive situations, which gives us power over that situation. We aren't doing it alone; we're partnering with God.

2. Tevet is a month to let go of anger concerning situations, those who've wronged us, and against ourselves. Survey what causes negative triggers. Triggers are often the first (unconscious) reactions we have in adverse circumstances. Many first express a form of anger. As you see those, take them and hand them to Jesus. Allow him to take them away in exchange for something better. If you don't know what to trade for, ask Jesus. He may give you something with an explanation of what to do with it.

3. As you see evil, practice releasing light into it. No darkness can stand in the presence of the light and glory of God.

4. Tevet is a month to see with our spiritual eyes. We learn how God is working in our lives to bring us to a level of maturity so we can teach

others. Practice exercising your spiritual eyes and journal about what you see.

5. Ayin is all about the eyes. In the month of Tevet, we look for the truth in our thoughts, intents, and behaviors. We also learn to see through God's eyes. With the eyes of your spirit, present yourself before God so you can view situations from his perspective. Take your thoughts, intents, and actions and hand them to him. Ask him to show you how he sees them.

   Tevet is a month of cleansing and purification. As we present ourselves before God, we learn how to clean the house of our soul. This is where unhealthy thoughts, intents, paradigms, and actions (behaviors) are swept out. Through the "eyes of God," we see a pathway from any darkness in our lives into the light.

Shevat שבט

Starts in January or February

Letter: *Tsadi* צ

Musical Note: *F-sharp*

> *Shevat* is the eleventh month on the Jewish calendar counting from Nisan. The high point of the month is the holiday of 15 Shevat, known as the 'New Year for Trees.' This is the day when the sap begins to rise in the fruit trees in Israel—the start of a new growing season. We mark the day by eating fruit, particularly from the 'Seven Kinds' with which Israel is blessed (wheat, barley, grapes, figs, pomegranates, olives and dates). On this day, we remember that 'Man is a tree of the field' and reflect on the lessons we can derive from our botanical analogue.[lvi]

Shevat is the month of silent new beginnings and the new year for trees. In a sense, it's an early start to spring. Trees are just coming out of a dormant period, even though on the surface, they still look as if nothing is happening! Judaism has several New Years, much like our calendar year (academic year, fiscal year, etc.) does. The 15th of Shevat is the beginning of the new year for the purposes of tithing fruit. As the trees shift into production mode, a spiritual shift of preparation for the upcoming fruitful season takes place.

The Torah has numerous verses comparing men to trees. As a side note, when photographed, our nervous system (via various medical techniques) looks like a tree! Our fruits are the deeds and expressions that come out of us. We might consider putting the old seasons behind and focusing on the new. During Shevat, the almond trees begin to blossom. They are the first bloomers, and the almond looks like an eye, so they are said to be "watcher" trees. In a sense, they keep watch for the spring.

Shevat is a shift month and steppingstone to the next place in our lives. We're coming from a dormant season into a fruit-bearing season. If we become too acquainted with the types and shadows of yesterday, we'll lie dormant.

It's time to consider Wisdom and what she must reveal to us in this season. New things can be a bit scary because we are wandering into the unknown. It's important not to let the unknown keep us from moving forward. This is where Wisdom and Counsel step in to help. As we engage with what they show us, we step from fear into faith, so we have the needed tools to move into the fruitful season. The aid of Wisdom and Counsel is likened to putting the best fertilizer on plants to promote healthier growth just as they're emerging from that dormant period. We weren't meant to take this journey alone. Enlist God's help as we look to Wisdom and Counsel to speak into us.

As I was saying about the eminent domain situation I was house hunting during Shevat. I could find absolutely nothing within my price range anywhere close to where I wanted to live and was about the appeal the state's decision a third time when a miracle happened. A house popped up on Craigslist of all places. It was in a location I hadn't previously considered, and after looking at it, I realized it was perfect. It required stepping into the unknown and trusting God to reveal the answer to my question, "Why this town?" There were so many unknowns as I moved forward with the purchase, but in my gut, I knew it was the right decision. If I had allowed fear to grip me, I might have missed this opportunity.

This is a great month to journal, although every month is good for that. When trees begin to bear fruit, there's often a lot of it, and sometimes it can rot before it's consumed. If we prepare ahead for this barrage of fruit, we'll know exactly what to do and how to handle all that comes with mighty fruit bearing.

Tsadi is the letter for Shevat. The original pictograph shows a man on his side. The gematria is ninety. The musical pitch is an F-sharp. The pictograph can also be a trail, which suggests a journey, chase, or hunt. This goes along with the sowing-and-reaping principle where justness and retribution play out. Tsadi can also be a reaping hook, pertaining to harvest. Tsadi means a righteous one, a leader and teacher of a generation. The gematria of ninety refers to being bent over in humility to God. Tsadi exists not for its own benefit but to serve God.[lvii]

Shevat Activation

1. Shevat is a season to think about coming out of dormancy. Look over the past three months to see what's been brewing in the darkness that's ready to bear fruit in the spring season. Begin preparing for the production mode of that fruit.

2. Invite Wisdom and Counsel to join you as you prepare for any unknowns during this preparatory season. If fear tries to rear its ugly head, go to your personal mountain and meet with Jesus. Have a discussion about how you can walk through the unknowns of this production season. From that place of rest, journal what you sense, see, hear, and feel.

3. Meditate on the shift during Shevat. See yourself on that steppingstone while preparing to move forward. Wisdom and Counsel will join you here.

4. Prepare for the sowing, reaping, and harvest season that's about to begin. Strategize with Jesus as to how that looks for you.

5. Tsadi is the only letter associated with the fundamental note, F-sharp. This note represents one of the most complex key

signatures in music. The letter Tsadi seems a bit complicated because it has many layers of meaning. We are invited to include wisdom and council into our lives during the month of Shevat.

The pictograph for the letter Tsadi depicts a man on his side in a position of humility. Throughout Shevat, imagine yourself in a place of humility before God amid the complicated layers of your life. Seek wisdom and counsel from that place to bring beautiful harmony as a frequency of expectancy into the "spring months" of your life. Bloom where you are planted!

Adar אדר

Starts in February or March

Letter: *Qoph* ק
Musical Note: *A-flat*

Adar is the twelfth month on the Jewish calendar counting from Nisan. "When Adar enters, joy increases," the Talmud says. Adar is a special month because it's a Jewish leap year. It occurs seven times in a nineteen-year cycle (approximately once every three years). There is an added month called "Adar I," inserted before this month of Adar (termed "Adar II" in leap years). This aligns the lunar months with the solar year, ensuring that the holidays fall in the proper seasons. Adar I is a *shanah meuberet* (i.e., a pregnant year).

"It is important to keep the calendars aligned for the festivals to retain their positions relative to the seasons as prescribed by the Torah. Adar is the official "happy month," as is written: "As soon as Adar begins, increase in joy!" In a leap year, we have two months of extra happiness! The festival of Purim, celebrated on Adar 14, is in Adar II in leap years, while the 14th of Adar I is marked symbolically as *Purim Katan*—Minor Purim."[lviii]

We're now coming out of the dark months so more light shines upon our lives and circumstances. As we look at the hidden things being revealed, it's a time to view more of our identity. We've taken inventory in some months. Now it's time to begin that forward motion into spring. Like a tree beginning to bud, we see more pieces of provision, our identity, and revelation about the next season. We release worry and focus on God's provision. His words are fertilizer for us so that we can grow into who we're called to be.

I moved into my new home during the month of Adar. It needed remodeling, which we did in the middle of several heavy snowstorms—going back and forth between two houses, three hours away from each other. Nothing about this move was easy. In a nutshell, I really needed revelation to answer the question, "What the heck am I doing?" While cleaning, painting, installing new flooring, and fixing other issues, I began to receive revelation concerning my lack of understanding as to why I had to move three hours away from a place I called home for a very long time. The key here is that I chose to move forward. That action opened the needed revelation.

Spring is the greatest time of growth for plant life. As I mentioned earlier, the Torah often refers to humans as trees. A tree looks very different in the colder months than it does during the warmer months. Cold months are for marinating and germinating over new things to be released in the seasons of plenty. Our problem often centers around how to release and walk in provision, our identity, and revelation. This is a preparation month for blooming so that good fruit can be produced in even the warmer months.

This month, reverse worry over finances, turn to faith and hope, and trust G-d to infuse us with the necessary nutrients so we can grow the most awesome fruit that can be eaten even during the lean months.

Qoph is the letter for Adar. The original pictograph is a circle with a line through it, depicting a sun on the horizon. The gematria is one hundred, and the musical note is A-flat. *Kuf* means "monkey." We hear the phrase "monkey see, monkey do." In a sense, Kuf is a mimic. It's also a coming around or a circuit of space or time. It's moving in a circle, which relates to the mimicking monkey. It goes on and on. A sun on the horizon indicates that morning is coming. This occurs daily, so it is indeed a circle of time. The gematria of one hundred is represented by both life and death. When making declarations and decrees of blessings, it replaces that which causes death.[lix]

Adar Activation

1. This is a month to let your light shine! We've come out of the dormant season. See yourself taking what you've learned in the hiddenness of the dark season of the past three months and bringing that into the light. As before, this comes from a place on the mountain of your life where you're in Christ. From this position, you see all that's below so you can move in a new direction. Be sure to journal how this looks and feels.

2. Begin to write and prepare more declarations and decrees specific to growth and bearing fruit as you move from growth and fruit-bearing to harvest.

3. Meditate on God's provision and his words, which are fertilizer for continual growth.

4. Release any fears and worries that accompany stepping into the unknown.

5. The Bible says that life and death are in the power of the tongue. (See Proverbs 18:21.) Release any death in your words by trading them for blessings that bring about life. Live this month with words of blessings over, in, and

through situations.

6. Qoph looks like a sun. It's also another circle of a continuous pattern. Engage with the "son" in the middle of this circle where light completely dispels darkness. Adar is the month before the beginning of another New Year. See yourself stepping into the light – a light that causes growth. Plants need sun to grow just like we need the "son" to grow into maturity.

   As we prepare for Nisan, we step into Qoph. In this place of light, we are in the center of God's name YHVH. When adding Jesus (the son), he stands in the center of God's name – YHSVH (Yod, Heh, Shin, Vav, Heh). In the center of anything, we receive the full light. Stand often in this center place. See yourself there – with Jesus – in the center of God's name.

References

[1]https://www.healingfrequenciesmusic.com/product/musical-frequencies-of-the-hebrew-letters/.
[2]https://www.healingfrequenciesmusic.com/product-category/song-of-the-month/.
[3] https://blog.freedom-flowers.com/times-seasons-healing-box/.
[4] John Stuart Reid, "Cymatics Experiment in the Great Pyramid," *Cymascope*, accessed September 30, 2019, https://www.cymascope.com/cyma_research/egyptology.html.
[5] Wikipedia, s.v., "archaeoacoustics," last modified June 27, 2019, https://en.wikipedia.org/wiki/Archaeoacoustics.
[6]https://www.youtube.com/user/SBResearchGroup/videos
[7] "Learn About the Scrolls," The Leon Levy Dead Sea Scrolls Digital Library, accessed September 30, 2019, https://www.deadseascrolls.org.il/learn-about-the-scrolls/introduction.
[8] Ibid.
[9] Jeff A. Brenner, "Ancient Hebrew Timeline," *Ancient Hebrew Timeline,* accessed September 30, 2019, https://www.ancient-hebrew.org/biblical-history/ancient-hebrew-timeline.htm.
[10] Tzvi Freeman, "What Is Kabbalah?: The Soul of Judaism," *Chabad*, accessed September 30, 2019, https://www.chabad.org/library/article_cdo/aid/1567567/jewish/Kabbalah.htm.

[11] Wikipedia, s.v., "Sefer Yetzirah," last modified September 26, 2019, https://en.wikipedia.org/wiki/Sefer_Yetzirah.
[12] Ibid.
[13] Bryan Griffith Dobbs, "Sefer Yetzirah: The Book of Formation," accessed September 30, 2019, http://www.faculty.umb.edu/gary_zabel/Courses/Phil%20281b/Philosophy%20of%20Magic/Arcana/Kabbalah/SeferYetzirah.htm.
[14] "Sepher Yetzirah – Book of Formation," *Hermetik International*, accessed September 30, 2019, https://www.hermetik-international.com/en/media-library/kabbalah/sepher-yetzirah-book-of-formation-saadia-version.
[15] Seneca Schurbon, *Healing in the Hebrew Months: Prophetic Strategies Hidden in the Tribes, Constellations, Gates, and Gems* (Idaho: Amazon, 2019).
[16] "Sepher Yetzirah," https://www.hermetik-international.com/en/media-library/kabbalah/sepher-yetzirah-book-of-formation-saadia-version/.
[17]https://www.healingfrequenciesmusic.com/product-category/song-of-the-month/.
[18] Wikipedia, s.v., "Richard Dumbrill (musicologist)," last modified September 18, 2019, https://en.wikipedia.org/wiki/Richard_Dumbrill_(musicologist).
[19] Richard Dumbrill, "Dumbrill on the Silver Lyre od Ur," YouTube, 35:15, September 11, 2018, https://youtu.be/e12hWw7R5CQ.
[20] MovieClips, "The Sound of Music (4/5) Movie CLIP - Do-Re-Mi (1965) HD," YouTube, 2:21,

September 28, 2015,
https://youtu.be/pLm07s8fnzM.
[21] Wikipedia, s.v., "concert pitch," last modified August 6, 2019,
https://en.wikipedia.org/wiki/Concert_pitch.
[22] John Opsopaus, "Some Notes on the History of Isopsephia (Gematria)," *Wisdom of Hypatia* , accessed September 30, 2019,
http://wisdomofhypatia.com/OM/BA/SNHIG.html.
[23]https://www.healingfrequenciesmusic.com/product/musical-frequencies-of-the-hebrew-letters/.
[24] Ibid.
[25]https://www.healingfrequenciesmusic.com/product-category/song-of-the-month/.
[26] www.healingfrequenciesmusic.com.
[27] "The Hebrew Month of Nisan," *Chabad*, accessed September 30, 2019,
https://www.chabad.org/library/article_cdo/aid/2164005/jewish/Nisan.htm.
[28] Rabbi Aaron L. Raskin, *Letters of Light – A Mystical Journey into the Hebrew Alphabet*, (New York: Sichos, 2012), 157, 159, 162.
[29] Ibid.
[30] "The Hebrew Month of Iyar," *Chabad*, accessed September 30, 2019,
https://www.chabad.org/library/article_cdo/aid/2198504/jewish/Iyar.htm.
[31] Schurbon, *Healing in the Hebrew Months.*
[32] Raskin, *Letters of Light*, 60, 62, 66.
[33] "The Hebrew Month of Sivan," *Chabad*, accessed September 30, 2019,
https://www.chabad.org/library/article_cdo/aid/2263473/jewish/Sivan.htm.
[34] Schurbon, *Healing in the Hebrew Months*, 26.

[35] Raskin, *Letters of Light,* 69, 72, 76.
[36] "The Hebrew Month of Tammuz," *Chabad,* accessed September 30, 2019, https://www.chabad.org/library/article_cdo/aid/2263474/jewish/Tammuz.htm.
[37] Schurbon, *Healing in the Hebrew Months.*
[38] Ibid.
[39] Raskin, *Letters of Light,* 80, 83–84.
[40] The Hebrew months use (at least) two numbering systems. The first one (used in this book) starts with Nisan in the Jewish New Year. The second system starts with the head of the year, Tishrei, and is when the number of the year changes (e.g., September 29, 2019, to September 18, 2020 is the Jewish year 5780).
[41] "The Hebrew Month of Av," *Chabad,* accessed September 30, 2019, https://www.chabad.org/library/article_cdo/aid/2263460/jewish/Av.htm.
[42] Raskin, *Letters of Light*, 90, 93–94.
[43] See footnote 39 on the two ways of numbering the Hebrew months.
[44] "The Hebrew Month of Elul," *Chabad*, accessed September 30, 2019, https://www.chabad.org/library/article_cdo/aid/3922314/jewish/About-the-Month-of-Elul.htm.
[45] Schurbon, *Healing in the Hebrew Months.*
[46] Raskin, *Letters of Light*, 100, 102, 106
[47] "The Hebrew Month of Tishrei," *Chabad*, accessed September 30, 2019, https://www.chabad.org/library/article_cdo/aid/2263462/jewish/Tishrei.htm.
[48] https://www.yourdreamventure.com/dream-ventures-discovery/.

[49] Raskin, *Letters of Light*, 120, 122, 124.
[50] "The Hebrew Month of Cheshvan," *Chabad*, accessed September 30, 2019, https://www.chabad.org/library/article_cdo/aid/2263464/jewish/Cheshvan.htm.
[51] Raskin, *Letters of Light*, 138, 142, 144.
[52] "The Hebrew Month of Kislev," *Chabad*, accessed September 30, 2019, https://www.chabad.org/library/article_cdo/aid/2263465/jewish/Kislev.htm.
[53] Raskin, *Letters of Light*, 148, 151, 153.
[54] "The Hebrew Month of Tevet," *Chabad*, accessed September 30, 2019, https://www.chabad.org/library/article_cdo/aid/2263466/jewish/Tevet.htm.
[55] Raskin, *Letters of Light*, 156, 159, 162.
[56] "The Hebrew Month of Shevat," *Chabad*, accessed September 30, 2019, https://www.chabad.org/library/article_cdo/aid/2099530/jewish/Shevat.htm.
[57] Raskin, *Letters of Light*, 174, 177.
[58] "The Hebrew Month of Adar," *Chabad*, accessed September 30, 2019, https://www.chabad.org/library/article_cdo/aid/2263483/jewish/Adar-Adar-II.htm.
[59] Raskin, *Letters of Light*, 186, 189–190.

About the Author

Del Hungerford

Del started her musical journey in beginning band at her elementary school. After fast forwarding through three music degrees (B.M., M.M., and D.M.A.), several school band teaching jobs, professional performing gigs, and teaching music at the college level, Del had some deep encounters with God that changed everything. Music—spontaneous creations from heaven—began to flow from within that wasn't on sheet music. This inspired her to research beyond normal academic ideas and religious protocols. Her spontaneous instrumental music is for sale on Amazon, CD Baby, iTunes, and her website, Healing Frequencies Music. Much of her research is documented in blog posts and videos (website and YouTube channel). When Del isn't creating music or researching, she enjoys spending time with her furry kitty friends, teaching music, or creating structures, such as door sheds, out of recycled materials.

Music website: www.healingfrequenciesmusic.com

Facebook: www.facebook.com/healingfrequenciesmusic

YouTube channel: www.youtube.com/user/Doxadelly

Supernatural Lessons website:

www.supernaturallessons.com

E-mail: info@healingfrequenciesmusic.com

Other Books by the Author

Accessing the Kingdom Realms

Follow Del on her personal journey of intimacy into the heart of the Father, Jesus, and Holy Spirit. While everyone's journey is uniquely their own, Del provides keys to help you cultivate a close relationship with each member of the Trinity. In this experiential book, you will find a map to guide you as you pursue the Trinity as well. Accessing Kingdom Realms is not just theory or head knowledge where you only dream about what you can do; it's about learning how to step into all that YHVH has for us here on earth today. All that's required is a willing, God-sanctified imagination. "Come up here!" says a voice from heaven. Read about Del's encounters, then activate your imagination to step deeper into the presence of YHVH. Worship at the throne, dance with the Father, and step into that intimate place as only a son or daughter can do.

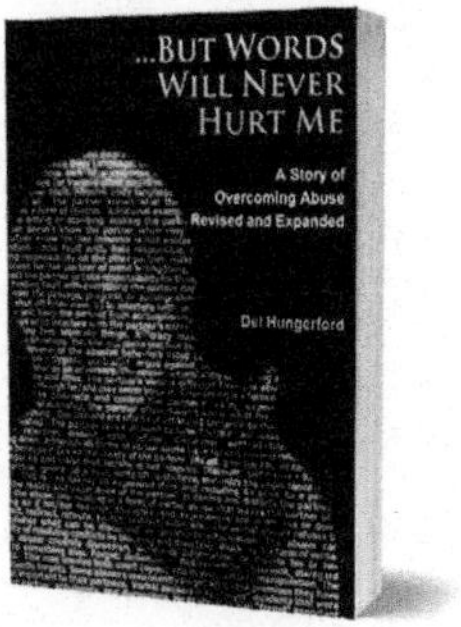

...But Words Will Never Hurt Me

... *But Words Will Never Hurt Me* is a story of overcoming abuse. It's from the perspective of the author who goes through her marriage wondering why everything is falling to pieces. The stories are reconstructed from journal entries with exact words between the couple, their friends, and their counselors. Del endeavors to allow the readers to make up their minds on what is going on in this marriage. After all, you can't try to put words in the mouth of someone other than oneself or explain another's feelings. Because of that, Del only shows what she feels, how she reacts, and provides insight into how she's affected by this relationship. Her husband's actions and words are described as they actually happened. However, there is no attempt to portray what he might have felt. The story ends with hope for the future. And, that one who has suffered at the hands of an abuser who didn't hit with fists, but with words, attitudes, indifference, and silence, can indeed overcome. "...But Words Will Never Hurt Me: A Story of Overcoming Abuse" is accompanied by a workbook that walks the reader through the various types of abuse so others, too, may find their way to a healthier life. The workbook is sold separately. For more information, visit the forum: www.freefromverbalabuse.com And visit the website: www.freefromverbalabuse.net

Accessing Your Spiritual Inheritance

It's Your Turn to Go Through the Door

Alice didn't fall down a rabbit hole but she did walk through a mystical doorway in a vision to recover blessings her ancestors failed to claim. When Alice came back and shared her experience, Seneca wasted no time going through her own door. Del's approach differed -- she wound up floating along in her bloodstream!

Through the map we give in our stories, others went through their own doors, leading to better relationships with God, increase in finances, favor, and giftings. Although this book touches on generational curses and how to remove them, we focus on claiming the blessings your family line has lost. However, you'll need to be open to having a vision, and we'll walk you through the step-by-step process of learning to see, so that you, too, can restore your lost generational blessings.
Your hidden inheritance awaits!

Made in the USA
Las Vegas, NV
24 February 2022

44514851R00089